Working for The Crew: Understanding Gang Controlled Sexual Exploitation

Deepa Patel, CSOTP, LCSW
and
Heather Peck, LCSW, BCD

To those that have wanted to speak but
have not

To those that have spoken and
been forgotten

There are some that will Always
Remember

FORWARD

Prostitution is often called the "oldest profession." Sexual exploitation has been in existence since probably the beginning of humankind. There are topics to be debated about a man or woman's right to choose how he or she uses his or her body. Is it really a "choice" when a woman impoverished, traumatized, sexually abused as a child enters a life of selling her body in a brothel? Is it a "choice" when a man lures a woman into selling herself to earn money for him under the guise of "everlasting love?" Is it a choice when a twenty-year-old brings a seventeen-year-old to a party, fills her full of alcohol and drugs and rapes her under the guise of "consensual sex?" Is it a choice when at sixteen years old, a male sells himself for food and shelter? Is it a choice when a woman, having been beaten and intimidated by a gang of men, sells herself to a buyer of sex because she doesn't have the psychological strength to run away instead?

For some of us who have chosen to work with men and women who are victims of sexual exploitation, these are very easy questions to answer, for others, maybe not. It depends on the lens through which you see, the knowledge you have about the business of sexual exploitation and the understanding you have of oppression, abuse, and manipulation.

The focus of this book is to provide information about the business of sexual exploitation through the lens of the victim. There will be a focus towards females being victimized from the perspective of gang controlled sexual exploitation. The goal is to inform in a manner that will assist you, the reader, to a conclusion about sexual exploitation. No hidden agenda here, we hope you will read this book, and agree that this is a heinous, horrifying, and vicious crime. There are no willing participants. There are traffickers, who are predators in whatever form they parade in pimp, boyfriend or gang member. There are victims, the women who exchange sexual acts, endure rape and violence, disease and poverty, to earn money for the men, women or family members they work for.

As authors, each have different areas of experience. Deepa Patel, CSOTP, LCSW is a pioneer in the field and has dedicated her professional life to addressing the treatment needs of gang controlled sexually exploited victims. She is a licensed clinical social worker and certified sex offender treatment provider. She has traveled throughout the world teaching, viewing the source of gang control, and advocating for victims. Deepa began her work before it became recognized as the scourge on the world that it is. She has worked with the exploiters, buyers, and victims of this business. She has been recognized for her expertise in the form of awards, White House visits, and consultation on a local, state and federal level but most rewarding for her is the victim who has an opportunity to be heard and who has the chance to heal.

Heather Peck, LCSW, BCD, DCSW is a seasoned clinician who has worked with victims for many years. Her experience with gang controlled sexual exploitation is as a child welfare administrator, clinical program developer, consultant, and as a seasoned veteran helping clinicians with various forms of compassion fatigue.

Ms. Patel and Ms. Peck are passionate about the need for victims to have a voice and an opportunity for a life that is safe and free of exploitation. Together, they have collaborated in the field, in trainings, and in program development. Their work has helped to solidify curriculums designed to provide comprehensive and concrete program and clinical skill development for helping professionals and paraprofessionals. These individuals include medical personnel, therapists, case managers, administrators, policy makers, and government officials. They both bring life experience to this book and offer it as a guide to a better understanding.

Be forewarned, the contents of this book are graphic, explicit, and often horrifying. It also offers solutions, hope, and resources for further understanding, support and guidance. Read, learn, question yourself and your motives for wanting to become involved in helping (if you dare), and recognize there are few rainbows, but those that appear, light up the Universe with such glory that it sustains us for another day.

Take a deep breath and read on.

CONTENTS

Introduction

Part 1
Veronica's Perfect Situation
Understanding Sexual Exploitation
Understanding Gangs
The Gang Controlled Game
Understanding Demand
Awakening and Understanding the Victims Mindset

Part 2
The Mental Health and Treatment Needs
Child Welfare
Collaboration
Compassion Fatigue
Special Thanks
Trauma and Hope
The Resilience Network
References

INTRODUCTION

In the last fifteen years, the area of gangs and sexual exploitation (also referred to as sexual abuse of children) has become an area of debate in practice and theory. Gang members are viewed as criminals. Female associates of gang members are known as the bad girls, the ones that get around, the ones that are difficult, trapped, and never getting out. Looking at it from another context, gang members and female associates often struggle with a lot of mental health complications as a result of their previous victimization. More than 90% of the gang controlled sexual exploitation victims have endured a traumatic event prior to their association with gang members. The majority of the gang-controlled exploitation victims are US Citizens.

These victims come from all different socio-economic classes, any gender, and ages range from childhood to adulthood. They come from two-parent homes, single parent homes, foster care, many different races, and those residing in some of the more gang-dominated communities, and those in million-dollar communities. The unsettling reality of offenders targeting juveniles and recruiting them into commercial sex enterprises has left victims in our society broken and in desperate need of help. Traffickers have become accustomed to exploiting individuals for their financial gain at any cost. That cost is usually an enormous amount of trauma induced by grooming, manipulation, and abuse which leave these children confused about themselves, their views of society and personal relationships. The abuse and trauma these victims are forced to endure causes both short-term and long-term implications for individuals, families, and communities.

While it is evident that sexual exploitation is an old problem, the current efforts to raise awareness and attention to the issue have been phenomenal. Can more efforts be made? Yes. However, something is better than nothing and the movement must continue, efforts need to be made, and change can be seen.

You purchased this book because something enticed you. Something motivated you, whether it was the cover or whether you were wondering what this Indian chick is talking about, YOU PICKED IT UP. That's change at its best.

To understand clearly a driving force to this book you have to focus on this………

You should know ahead of time; this book was written by non-traditional therapists. To understand this population, you have to think outside the box and standard norms do not apply.

The following is a driving factor provided by Deepa:
Friday, December 1, 2017. I'm sitting at home listening to a rerun of Jersey Shore, all my writing is out in front of me and I am organizing this very book for print. A client I have known since she was 15 calls to update me. She tells me how she studied and got an A in math on a test at a prestigious university. She proceeds to tell me how excited she was because she studied, tried and did it. I joke with her about a question I've asked her since she was 15 and in a math class in high school. Through the course of the conversation Veronica says:

Veronica: I needed to do this class to help me learn how to do my taxes early…..Ms. Deepa, I'm not one of those fools waiting until the last minute to pay taxes. I'm staying ahead.
Deepa: I'm about to cry girl, do you know……..

(in a politely rude manner Veronica cuts me off)

Veronica: I know, I know Ms. Deepa if I got through my shit.....Big Girl problems are a joke. Veronica then jokes and says "you turning up tonight?"
Deepa: Haha, no I am finishing up that book we discussed.
Veronica: Good, you scared about it?
Deepa: Yea, but it makes me want to work harder and get it done
Veronica: Good. You better do it Ms. Deepa. You can do it. Say something for those that didn't. All that stuff seems to be forgotten.

Veronica's drive is similar to many of the clients I have worked with over the years and will continue to work with.

VERONICA'S PERFECT SITUATION

Almost your typical middle-class home
Madre wasn't home
And padre? Well- he was in the jail cell long gone

Mom had to provide for the family
So to help her out she and Veronica moved out and lived with her extended family

Grandmother who thinks her precious baby girl can become anything in the world
Grandfather old school
Pretty much is the center of the cycle of abuse

Mother looking for love bringing other men home
Veronica sees it all the time - the mother just doesn't have time - so Veronica's often left alone

Grandfather steadily molesting her
Steadily undressing her
Started off with him kissing and caressing her
Eventually sexing her

And what's Veronica gonna say?
Her mother tries to be blind to the signs of her grandfather, who is her mother's father who did her the same way

Veronica is vulnerable and scared so much
Barely leaves a room because her eyes are red from her crying so much

Turns to social media for all of her satisfaction

How many likes she gets is her definition of a good interaction

Poor self-esteem
She's in the perfect situation as a guy sees her alone as she is leaving her class
And approaches and asks her if she wants to make some extra cash

UNDERSTANDING SEXUAL EXPLOITATION

QUIET NOISE
(Statistics)
Can I call your attention
To a situation that isn't getting much attention?

This very Nation - is facing a crisis called sexual exploitation
And the purpose of this is for a discussion to start generating
It's disgusting that it's happening over generations

12 million victims worldwide
And probably a whole lot more that have gone unidentified
This isn't fake news - so the truth we have to express
This needs to be addressed
Because over 100,000 children are victims in the US

Ages 12-14 - they prey on those from broken homes and with low self-esteem

Providing them with access to drugs and alcohol
Monetary gains, fame, they'll promise it all

Whatever it takes for them to get what they need to get
Many live by the code so they won't ever confess to it
It's a modern-day slave type deal
They recruit you promising they will provide and help make sure your problems are subsidized type deal
And it's not like you can always "Just say no"
Sometimes it's either say yes or watch members of your family go

*Force fraud or coercion are main methods to win you over
Don't want you to be scared or look over your shoulders
But they are at lots of places- looking for runaways all over*

At bus stops, shopping malls, hang out spots, school halls

Or even where you stay

Human Trafficking is one of the largest criminal industries in the world. The terms, human trafficking and sexual exploitation are frequently used interchangeably. The federal Trafficking Victims Protection Act defines the crime of human trafficking as "A. The recruitment, harboring, transportation, provision, or obtaining of a person for the purpose of a commercial sex act where such an act is induced by force, fraud, or coercion, or in which the person induced to perform such act has not attained 18 years of age, or B. For labor or services, through the use of force, fraud, or coercion for the purpose of subjection to involuntary servitude, peonage, debt bondage, or slavery" (Matter, Journal)

Human trafficking, particularly in the form of sexual exploitation, is the fastest growing criminal enterprise in the world. The current reports suggest that the gross profit from this illegal activity has surpassed that of firearms trafficking and is rapidly approaching that of narcotics trafficking. It is essential to keep in mind that neither sex trafficking nor labor trafficking refers solely to foreign nationals within the United States, rather a vast majority of exploitation victims are in fact US citizens. Slavery is termed as property bought and sold and forced to work. It is a system still prevalent in America today, and we see that in the exploitation of adults and children. Sexual exploitation of youth is child sexual abuse in whatever form that may take. Exploitation is defined by federal law as the exchange of sexual activity for any tangible or intangible good such as necessary food, clothing, shelter, material possessions, drugs, or money. Regardless of the form or alleged willingness of the youth to participate in sexual activity, or the alleged response of the victim while engaged in the sexualized action, this is child sexual abuse. There are a variety of forms of sexual exploitation including gang controlled sexual exploitation, familial exploitation, forced marriage, pimp-controlled exploitation, and survival sex.

Force, fraud, and coercion are three critical elements when it comes to Sexual Exploitation

It is imperative to understand why sexual exploitation is growing at such a rapid rate. One of the reasons is that it is a high yield, low-risk enterprise. In the illegal drug industry, one must purchase a lot of drugs and may have other individuals assist them to cut, count, bag, and distribute. The profits are mostly shared. The product is completed and then they must purchase an additional supply. However, a trafficker can make a high profit for sexually exploiting a minor by grooming them, coercing them to engage in sexual acts for money, and then collecting an income. The benefits are not shared. The trafficker's mentality focuses on the victim as a product that can be re-used multiple times in one day, seven days a week. If the trafficker is exploiting multiple victims, that multiplies his/her gain even further. These victims do not have to continuously be replaced or re-purchased such as in the weapons or drug industry. They are considered "renewable resources" that often require little to no investment. Traffickers have made it their profession and are dedicated to discovering new ways to recruit victims. If they were to lose a victim, he/she could probably be replaced the next day, and business goes on as usual. The population they are targeting is also one of the most vulnerable which makes it that much more simple to maintain an influx of victims.

In the context of the victims, their background before meeting a trafficker can be horrific.

Every year, there are approximately 1.7 million runaway/throwaway incidents in the U.S., and about 90%

of runaways become involved in the sex trade industry (Priebe & Suhr, 2005). In most cases of victims who have been sexually exploited, there was an extensive history of running away (Priebe & Suhr, 2005). These children are often running away to escape a negative home environment, trauma, neglect, or other mental health-related concerns, but unfortunately land into the arms of a person wanting to make a profit and posing as a protector and caretaker (Smith et al., 2009). For most of the victims, living in dysfunction, anywhere, is better than home; even if others view it as more dangerous. To the victims, they view it as safer than the past and can often attain a better feeling. To the victims, they can sometimes feel as if they are in control.

We are all wired to love, bond, and connect. For the most vulnerable and often already victimized, when this is not present in the home they will find it somewhere else. An article featured in *Psychology Today* entitled "How Love Controls Us," explains the concept that one-way love (unrequited love) or rejected/abandoned love, can wreak havoc on the impacted person's serotonin levels. They display significant drops in serotonin as high as 40%, according to research by Donatella Marazziti (K. Key, *Psychology Today,* 2011). Serotonin is a substantial contributor to happiness and well-being. Therefore if it is reduced at such significant levels, especially in adolescents in these situations, it will most likely set the stage for depression and affect mood stabilization. Once the trafficker offers that sense of love and connection everything changes. The article further explains that the biological underpinnings of love reveal that the early stages of falling in love (or infatuation) trigger a release of the feel-good neurotransmitter dopamine. This increase of dopamine creates feelings of exhilaration, heightened focus, and increases one's energy. This explains why, when people are falling in love, they might lose weight, become more active, stay up all night talking with each other, and feel euphoric as if they're walking on a cloud (K. Key, Psychology Today 2011). Once the victim has been groomed, the victimization of sexual exploitation takes places.

In many cases, especially before the spread of exploitation awareness, the victims were the ones being arrested and charged with "prostitution" and other crimes while the traffickers, as well as the "Johns" (consumers), were getting away with exploitation and purchasing sex from minors. The criminalization of victims must stop and those preying on the vulnerabilities should be held accountable.

Research has demonstrated that negative home life experiences are a significant predictor for sexual exploitation (Priebe & Suhr, 2005). Conflict in the home can be caused by parental neglect, physical and sexual abuse, parental drug use, housing instability, and violence (Priebe & Suhr, 2005). This dysfunctional type of family life often provides a greater incentive for many individuals to leave home. A case example could include a child raped by her biological father and then sexually abused by her older half-brother. Home would not be a safe place and her self-worth would begin to break down. This would make her an easy target for traffickers and would make 'selling the story' easier.

Victims who have experienced emotional and psychological difficulties are at a greater risk for being sexually exploited (Priebe & Suhr, 2005). These girls often experience symptoms of depression, post-traumatic stress, anxiety, oppositional defiant disorder, reactive attachment disorder, etc. These conditions can impair their ability to have sound judgment and make good choices. In many cases, adolescents who aren't correctly diagnosed or treated for their psychological or emotional problems will ultimately try and self-medicate in any way they can. This can be either through substance abuse, high-risk behaviors or promiscuity.

Many people will confuse promiscuity with exploitation and use the terms interchangeably, however, this is not the case. Many victims of exploitation are seen as promiscuous and are often referred to as "sluts, hood rats or hoes." When someone is being exploited, they are being used for sex against their will in exchange for monetary or material gain that benefits the trafficker. Fear, force, and coercion also play a role and are key in distinguishing the two terms. There is a level of grooming involved. Grooming is best defined as the process in which a trafficker begins a subtle preparation process to gain the victims love, loyalty, and respect.

Grooming can begin with showering the victim with expensive gifts, clothing, etc. The victim then begins to see and trust this man as a "companion' or 'boyfriend.' The relationship soon becomes sexual and more intense. There is also a purely psychological component to grooming where the trafficker begins to slowly isolate and disassociate the victim from the world in which they know. The ultimate goal is for the victim to have the complete and total dependency on his/her trafficker. This process will ultimately lead to isolating the victim from friends and family as well.

The following portrays the process in which grooming can occur:

The grooming described above transitions into the 'seasoning' process which is now preparing the victim for 'the life.' The trafficker may begin to physically abuse the victim to 'toughen her up' and exert force and control. The trafficker can become aggressive, sexually abusive, and possibly degrading to acquire compliance and prepare the victim for engaging in sexual acts with the buyers.

Lastly, supply and demand. Sex sells and always will. There will always still be buyers. As long as there continue to be accessible targets for traffickers to recruit, groom and market for sex, the cycle will continue. Whether it is the victim, perpetrator, buyer, myself, school teacher, officer, judge, gas station attendant or hostess, we all have vulnerabilities. Unfortunately, for some, preying on those vulnerabilities fulfills that individual's needs.

Yo see that girl over there?
Yeah you see the that one with the nice body long brown hair
I'm telling u - I can get her first and sell her to y'all for cheap
Give me about a few weeks and I'll let you know the fee
You see

I'm real smooth with words and I got money to back it up
I'm goin ask the OG to let me borrow his truck
And by the end of the week I'm gonna pick babygirl up
And sho' nuff

He ran over to her and started talking giving tons of compliments
Asking to carry her books to class, time in the cafeterias they spent
Told her his parents were rich and had a couple of homes out for rent

Said he wanted to give her the world
He was always dreaming of this type of girl
And she was certainly his type
He was talking time together always and forever - make her his wife
And she believed it all
Because she came from a broken family and the amount of people who were nice to her was small

And before the week was up
Came out of school and while in mid strut
Heard the horn beep twice and there he was waiting for her in the truck

She was awestruck
Went on a ride
Then he got inside

She complied
He could see the love in her eyes

Told you
I could do it - it was really nothing to it
They say if You want something in life – you have to pursue it
So what's up?
$200 and I'll get her to let you fuck

She's uneasy at first but when he promises to buy her
purses, boots, jeans, and skirts
She lifts up her skirt and says "fine tell them I'm in"
And let the cycle begin

UNDERSTANDING GANGS

The gang epidemic has been a phenomenon in America. The earliest attention towards what is now being described as gangs was in 1700's but was more focused towards young people being a nuisance. Over the last few decades, gangs have evolved and continue to do so. Children as young as five are being noticed in elementary schools doodling gang signs or drawing. Gangs have spread to new areas, evolved over the years, and continue to grow.

To understand gang controlled sexual exploitation, you have to understand the operation and system of gangs. There are several key factors to understanding what constitutes a gang, how gangs function, and what their overall mentality is. All of these factors significantly impact the treatment of victims of commercial sexual exploitation by gangs, and it is imperative that those working with these victims have a working knowledge of the aspects of life that the victim experienced during their exploitation. It should be noted that individuals who have been exploited in the commercial sex trade by gangs often adopt the various means and methods of representing gang affiliation as the gang by which they are exploited. Recognizing how a gang represents itself will greatly increase one's ability to determine if there is potential gang affiliation regarding the client.

In building a firm foundational knowledge of gangs, let us first establish a definition of a gang. Many states have passed gang-related legislation, which varies from state, but all embody the same core principles. Those principles suggest that a gang:
1. Is a group of three or more persons who band together;
2. The common purpose is engaging in criminal conduct;

3. The group has adopted, as a means of identifying itself, a common name, sign, or symbol to represent the group.

This definition, arguably, is very broad and lends itself to encompass many different groups that may not, by common definition or understanding, be considered a gang. Based on the various forms of representation adopted by these gangs, it is important for persons assessing for possible gang membership to pay attention to the style of dress, tattoos, clothing, hand signs, drawings, etc. It should be noted that multiple factors should be considered when thinking about asking questions regarding gang affiliation. Assumptions regarding gang affiliation can impact relationships with individuals. Gangs, by their nature, consume the life of the participant. Regardless if it is a male/female seeking initiation into the gang or a female who will ultimately be exploited by the gang, the gang utilizes the same methodologies of indoctrination to change the person's worldview around them. Gangs exploit the vulnerabilities of the individual to convince them to leave behind their biological family and adopt the gang as their new family.

It is important to understand the origin of gangs. There are two primary reasons that gangs have historically formed, in response to poor socio-economic conditions or for protection. It is important to note as a central theme to all gangs that these groups were specific to the community or neighborhood in which they lived. Their efforts at obtaining resources were to serve the needs of their particular community. Within those communities, these groups were respected as the protectors and providers of the neighborhood. Thus began their taste of power and control. As the gangs continued to evolve, they learned that more profit could be obtained through the sale of illegal narcotics. As a result, gangs become increasingly self-servicing and began to be more seeking of a lucrative criminal entity and less for intervening in helping respective communities.

Due to the presence of illegal narcotics, once again a decline occurred in the economic and substantial resources within the community, and the inherent increase in drug addiction violence become an unavoidable consequence. The escalation of violence within these communities spiraled out of control and where once power and control were about respect, it turned to be more about fear because they controlled the majority of the financial resources within the community. Gangs also increasingly added weapons as a means of control. Groups that started within the goals of bettering their community and providing for those that could not provide for themselves, quickly became money hungry and extremely violent terrorists within their communities, controlling the people living there through fear and intimidation. There was no escaping the control of the evolved criminal street gangs. The only option was submission, enabling the gangs to grow in strength. Eventually, these gangs began to expand into many of the national gangs that are presently thriving in many cities throughout the United States.

Ironically, the other reason why gangs came into existence was for protection. Many of the gangs that have been birthed here in the United States were a direct result of the need for protection from other gangs or groups threatening the safety of local communities. Gangs, regardless of whether they are transnational, national, or local crews, remain extremely territorial, a concept which is essential to understanding the operation of gangs in the realm of commercial sexual exploitation.

The concept of power and control drives the gang member and his/her way of thinking. Some might anecdotally say that gang members are 'drunk on power.' The methodology of reasoning becomes skewed and the survival and prosperity of the gang becomes central to the gang member's life. Every aspect of their life is motivated by the concept of "gang over all." This can be best explained by considering the concept of self-preservation. In times of crisis, the body will naturally move into a defensive mode where all efforts are taken to ensure the survival of the individual. Many times, the mind will cause the person to abandon efforts to assist others in need during this period of the crisis, until some sense of balance can be established and ordinary reasoning is restored. The gang itself takes on the form of self-preservation and the gang member adopts the survival of the gang mentality as equally important, if not more important, than personal survival. In this way, the gang takes precedence over self, family, community, faith, or any other influence in one's life. Commitment and dedication to the gang can be appropriately described as nothing less than extreme and unhealthy, particularly when this level of influence and indoctrination occurs during key developmental periods in an adolescent's life.

Another concept that is important to understand when dealing with gang-involved persons is the idea of "blood in and blood out." " Blood in" means that the person has to shed blood, usually through an initiation process involving some form of physical assault to become a member. Since the person shed his/her blood to become a member of the gang, the gang now runs through his/her blood. The person is expected to leave the former life behind (including biological family) and adopt the gang family as the center of his/her life. "Blood out" means that one must also shed blood to leave the gang. This time it is more dramatic because the belief is that since the gang now runs through his/her blood, he/she must shed all their blood to be free of the gang truly. This means that one can only be free from the gang at death. Anyone being indoctrinated or initiated into the gang accepts this fictitious notion as truth and a code to live by. The depth of this indoctrination is very complex and requires intensive attention to be paid to these issues before one can truly understand why gang members stay in the lifestyle, get out of the lifestyle and control others out of fear.

Gangs thrive on violence. The level of violence is augmented by societal changes in today's culture. Violence is accepted more regularly among our young people as it has become common place on television, in the movies and video games, as well as lyrics in popular songs. The desensitization of American society to violence, coupled with the pack mentality that exists among gang members, enables gangs to carry out acts of violence that are much more barbaric than someone with a balanced understanding of right and wrong would be able to commit.

Traditionally, violence has been viewed as the central driving ideology of gang life. However, as more instances of profit-driven crime surface, particularly the commercial sexual exploitation of persons, we now understand more fully that the violence is only a means to an end. The violence helps the gangs to establish the power and control that they are seeking. This power and control is seen as respect by the gang members, but it is known that it is truly just a manifestation of fear and dominance. Recalling that gangs are very territorial, they gain control over territory (neighborhood or community) through showing people living within their sphere of influence that they are capable of delivering physically punitive repercussions if the requests and rules of the gang are not followed. This deters residents from reporting criminal activity to law enforcement or even cooperating with law enforcement investigations. The neighborhood and operations of the gang are thus shielded from interdiction and dismantling by authorities.

Fundamentally gangs can be broken down into three categories:

Transnational Gangs

These are gangs that are connected to other countries. Examples of these gangs include Mara Salvatrucha (MS13) and 18th Street. These gangs began in the United States but migrated to other countries for various reasons. These gangs have a hierarchical structure and it is known that often these borders do not interfere with the communication between various members and "cliques" or "sets" of the gang. Cliques, or sets, are smaller subsets of the gang that can be specific to a geographical area. These smaller subsets have their hierarchical structure as well, but still report their activities and take direction from the larger gang leadership. Leadership within these transnational gangs is typically well-defined and there are consequences for not following the rules or directions of the leadership.

It should be noted that these gangs are highly adaptable and mobile depending on their environment. It is a priority to conceal them from detection from law enforcement. Across the country, law enforcement has become more effective in identifying and prosecuting gang members for criminal behavior. Many of these suppression efforts have caused gangs to move behind closed doors and away from their former visibility on the street corners. They have moved away from the colors, markings, etc., but this does not mean gangs are not as identifiable as they once were. These gangs remain extremely violent and aggressively territorial. Their criminal operations are distinctive, productive, and protected by other members of the gang.

With regards to these transnational gangs, in an effort to distance the gang name from the criminal conduct, a shift has been noted wherein most of the illegal activity is carried about by persons that have not yet attained membership status. These individuals, who are in what can be described as a probationary period, are directed by the leadership of the gangs to carry out illegal activities which further the overall mission of the gang. Different groups provide different names for these people; some examples are "probe," "chequeo," and "paisa." It is important to understand that when someone carries this status, they have already begun the process of indoctrination, and internally they feel that they are in fact a member and carry the same level of loyalty and commitment, if not even greater, to the gang as a full-fledged member.

National Gangs:
National gangs are gangs that exist primarily here in the United States. However, their presence can be seen in multiple states spanning from the east coast to the west coast and many states in between. Some common examples of national gangs are those like the Bloods and Crips. Similar to transnational gangs, national gangs have a distinct hierarchical structure of leadership and there are known consequences for not following the rules or directions of leadership. Additionally, it is common among these national gangs to have their rules in written form. Some of these criminal enterprises have attempted legitimization for their criminal operations through legalized incorporation.

National gangs will adopt a multitude of signs and symbols that represent their criminal enterprise. Recognizing some of these symbols is key to recognizing gang affiliation. National gangs also tend to adopt various forms of dance and secret handshakes as a means of representation. National gangs are also broken down into subsets within the gang. Often these subsets are in communication across state lines and can come together to form a multi-state criminal enterprise where each subset supports the other's operations. These gangs are characterized as being well established with the capability of delivering extreme levels of calculated violence. Because of the organization of these criminal street gangs, they most resemble higher levels of organized crime such as the mob or mafia. They have shifted from street-level operations to becoming very business-oriented in their approach to criminal conduct.

National gangs tend to send their younger members, typically juveniles, into the streets to carry out gang business. The reasoning behind this is because the gangs know that juvenile members are more influenced by the desire to be accepted by the gang and are willing to carry out more risky tasks. Additionally, they know that if a juvenile is interdicted by law enforcement that the penalties for their criminal conduct will be much more lenient through the juvenile justice system. It can be argued that often these people also become victims of the gang, although not always used for commercial sexual exploitation; they are exploited because of other vulnerabilities and their legal status and age.

Hybrid/Local Gangs
These are the most overlooked gangs because they do not self-identify. They may call themselves a "crew" or could explain that they are simply "hood reppin." "Hood Reppin" can best be explained as gang's verse for representing the neighborhood where the gang lives. For example, take a group living in an apartment complex called Kingsley Commons. That group would adopt the name "Kingsley Commons" or some derivative thereof. If one were to question a member, he/she might explain that they are simply displaying pride in the neighborhood in which they live. Despite the self-identification, the fact is the group still meets criteria for a criminal street gang.

These groups tend to be smaller in membership and have varied life spans. It is possible that they will last for a long period, but it is also possible that they will exist for only a few months until they are absorbed into a larger gang or dismantled by collaborative efforts of law enforcement and stakeholders. These groups are routinely dismissed as not having the ability to carry out the same level of criminal conduct as the larger gangs.

Regardless of whether a gang is transnational, national, or local, each gang follows a standard pattern of growth. Understanding how these gangs develop helps to determine the probability of whether they are involved in exploitation. Studying gangs across the United States has shown that this pattern applies to gangs moving into new territory or gangs that are just forming. Looking at where the gang is developmentally will yield information on the scope of its existence.

The first step for a gang is to determine its sphere of control. They will need to decide what neighborhood or geographical area they are going to claim as "their territory." They will need to mark territory visually so that competing groups will be aware of the declared borders. The established method of doing so is through the use of graffiti. Members will 'tag' or place graffiti on buildings or other landmarks that fall within their territory. During this period, the gang will also establish the majority of their identifying names, signs, and symbols. Studying graffiti associated with various gangs provides a wealth of insight into the gang, how they view themselves and provide clues for warning signs in the future for recognizing potential gang affiliation. A simplistic example of this would be if all of the gang's markings are blue in color, then it would be a fair assumption that the gang will represent affiliation and has adopted the color blue.

There are two general types of graffiti; gang graffiti, and tagger graffiti. The primary difference between the two is that gang graffiti is used to mark territory or communicate messages between members or gangs. Gang graffiti is simplistic and usually comprised of straight line diagrams or simple words, letters, or numbers. In comparison, tagger graffiti tends to be much more artistic. There are various types of tagger graffiti that exist, but the purpose is not to mark territory, but rather a product of creative expression. Graffiti is a manner of speech and identification for the gangs. This is not limited to just physical structures.

Gang members have evolved with technology and have begun to represent their affiliation on social media. There is a wealth of knowledge to be acquired when access is gained to social media accounts used by the gang. They will not only display pictures of signs and symbols associated with the gang, but a review of the person's contacts will reveal associations with other gang members as well. Members will also post pictures of possible weapons in their possession, identify various crimes that they may be involved in, and discuss various recruitment efforts. Outside of social media, there are several other open source sites online such as YouTube that will assist in gathering intelligence relative to gangs. During the period that the gang is starting to establish its identity within the community, there will also be a notable rise in petty crime, crimes which are sometimes mislabeled as juvenile delinquency. These include activities such as theft, destruction, disorderly conduct, or alcohol violations.

Once pressure has been established, the gang will need to defend the territory which they claim to control. At this stage in the evolutionary process, the escalation of violence begins. It typically manifests itself through simple assaults occurring after school or in the early evening hours. The types of crimes being perpetrated by the gang move from behavioral to more predatory. The gang needs to share its identity with the community, draw attention to their presence, and defend their name. All of this also begins the process of reinforcing the concept of the false understanding of power and respect that makes up the gang mentality.

As a criminal enterprise, the gangs are limited in options as to how they can make money. The most common forms of profitable crimes that gangs engage in are extortion, narcotics, firearms trafficking, and sex trafficking. Of these four, sex trafficking is the highest yield with the lowest risk of criminal prosecution. The gangs have established power and control over the neighborhoods, so now they are free to essentially 'set-up shop' without fear of reports to law enforcement. Residents will be non-responsive to law enforcement because of the fear of retaliation.

Risk Factors for Gang Membership
Gang members are known to come from broken, dysfunctional homes and resort to gang membership for a vast number of reasons. Many are looking for protection or a sense of belonging/identity. Some are in search of an escape from their home life and a 'new family.' Below are some of the most common risk factors:

    -History of physical/sexual abuse
    -Lack of family support
    -Habitual runaway
    -Truant in school
    -Lacking self-worth
    -Substance abuse
    -Mental health issues (undiagnosed or misdiagnosed)

Now there is a clear understanding that as it relates to adolescent gang members, I have worked with over the years, majority of which have experienced some traumatic event.

It should be noted that risk factors for victims of trafficking often overlap with risk factors for gang membership, similar to their recruitment tactics. These victims are often habitual runaways as well, have been physically and sexually victimized, and are looking for an escape. It should also be noted that gang membership/victimization is not limited to these factors and gang members have been seen through high socioeconomic environments.

Gang Recruitment
There are many allures to gang life, but it is important to know that in each case, the gang is exploiting some vulnerability of the potential member or victim. Whether gangs are recruiting for new members or the purposes of exploitation, they seek to take advantage of specific vulnerabilities that serve as predominant driving factors in the social and psychological developmental process of the youth. Recruitment can be done in many venues; some include the neighborhoods where the gangs operate. It is also done quite regularly through the use of social media. Most gangs do not recruit arbitrarily, but instead, focus their recruitment efforts based on gathered intelligence on intended targets. Gang members will use social media sites to collect and compile this 'intelligence' on finding vulnerable individuals and then targeting their victims.

The majority of juveniles recruited into gangs are done so by someone known to the recruited. This is often done in the form of peer pressure. It is well known that peer pressure can be a very powerful motivator. Many youth are drawn into gangs because they feel that 'everyone else is doing it' or at the minimum, their friends are involved.

Another strategy exploited by the gangs is offering the youth a sense of belonging. Many children in today's society lack a stable support structure in the home. This can be a result of varying factors, but it ultimately results in the youth seeking out a group that can provide an identity to the child. The child is then manipulated into believing that the gang family is their new family, replacing the presence, influence, and role of the biological family.

Some are recruited into gangs merely because they live in the neighborhood where the gang operates. Recognizing that gangs are very territorial, we know that their sphere of control is typically limited to the community in which they live and work their criminal enterprises. Within these geographical areas, gangs will also recruit. Therefore, it is only reasonable to expect recruitment efforts to be targeted on young people who live in that area.

Socioeconomic reasons, while not the most predominate reason people join gangs, remain a noteworthy motivating factor for gang membership. At times youth exposed to situations of poverty are lured into the gang lifestyle through promises of money and material possessions.

Due to the perceived power and control that gangs have there is a belief that gangs can provide protection. In a society where the problem of "bullying" has become an increasing area of concern, youth are addressing the issue through various means. Experts in the field draw attention to the rise in teen suicide, substance abuse, and mental health issues as being directly linked to bullying. However, another response that some youth have is allying themselves with individuals or groups that can provide that protection for them against would-be bullies. Often we see, through the empowerment of gangs, the victim becomes the offender in situations which he/she justifies as only self-preservation and defense.

Some of today's youth are drawn to the adrenaline rush that comes from participating in pack-driven criminal conduct. The notion is planted in the minds of children through various forms of media, not limited to just television, movies, music, and video games. These adrenaline based fantasies presented to youth creates a desire to live out the scenarios; often leaving the child unfulfilled or disappointed, leading to more increasingly dangerous risk-taking behavior. Some are simply seeking fun and excitement. Adolescents view the gang lifestyle of being filled with endless parties and no stress or external pressures to perform well in school. Others might seek the gang life for access to drugs and alcohol which otherwise might be unattainable. For teenage boys, they could potentially join because of the social status associated with gang membership, including giving them access to females. Those that may be bullied in school could seek gang affiliation for their personal protection.

When working with gang members or gang-affiliated youth, it is important to have an understanding of the differences between gangs, particularly those that are rivals. As part of the gang culture, there needs to be an understanding that rivals are a great threat. A gang member at any point can be provoked, attacked, or killed for no reason. In a controlled setting, a gang member can refuse to sit at a table or even enter a room where there is a rival gang member. If precautions are not taken within a residential setting to control situations like this, the safety of residents, as well as staff, is jeopardized. Ensuring that the proper precautions and measures are taken when serving this population can help control this.

Female Gangs
Female gang membership has been on the rise in the past ten years. Much research has ignored female gang membership, which could be attributed to most believing the roles of females in the gang were minimal. However, over the years, females involvement within the gang context has risen and females are assuming the same

purpose and responsibilities as males. It should be noted that female gang membership is dependent on the gang. Transnational gangs are whereas less likely to have females as full-fledged members, where national and local gangs are more inclined. Females are often underestimated but should not be taken lightly as they are capable of committing the same crimes and are often connected to gang members and leaders for whom they carry out different tasks. The males use women because they used to be less likely to be searched and arrested by police. These females are extremely loyal to the gang and therefore just as dangerous.

The most famous case of female gang membership that gained national and international attention was the Brenda Paz case. Brenda was a female MS13 gang member who was sent to Virginia by one of her leaders to start a branch of MS13 in the area. Brenda, however, was about to face murder charges for a hit conducted by MS13 in another locality. She chose to cooperate with the police and in exchange, she would not be charged. Brenda became one of the FBI's most useful informants in the gang world. The information she gave assisted the FBI in solving more than 50 unsolved gang-related cases. She also gave the FBI precious and sensitive information regarding MS13.

While in witness protection, Brenda could not deter her gang affiliation. She returned to Virginia and began associating with MS13 once again. MS13 members realized that Brenda had been cooperating with law enforcement and murdered her. She had repeatedly been stabbed and nearly decapitated. This story is famous within the gang culture as gangs often emphasize Brenda's story of promoting loyalty, secrecy and the consequence to breaking the bond of gangs.

Generational Gangs

Generational gangs are individuals where gang membership has occurred throughout the family system. An example would be a father that is gang involved teaching and enforcing gang dynamics with their children. Historically, gangs serve the purpose of fulfilling a sense of family. Generational gangs are family members that have been gang-involved and passed that trait through their family. They are the most challenging cycle of gang membership to break due to their immediate family being involved. For the cycle of generational gangs to be broken, a separation from the family must occur.

THE GANG CONTROLLED GAME

INSIDE PERSPECTIVE
I'm a member of a powerful gang
Money drugs cars weapons we have everything
And I'm used to getting what I want- I'll do anything
And I've got my eyes on this pretty young thing

See- I've been watching her for a while now so I know
That her mom works two jobs so after school nobody is really home
and that's the only place she really goes
And I can tell from her social media posts
That she would love a brand new set of clothes
And I know
If I buy her a pair of new sneaks
She'll be in love with me in a few weeks

Sure enough
Bought her some outfits and stuff
Now she's over every day hanging with the gang and stuff

Need a few dollars and know someone who's interested in her type
Says he'll give a good amount if she comes and stays the night
At first, she says "Hell no" starts to fuss and fight
I tell her "if you love me you'll do it" - and I make sure she gets high as a kite
Nobody else provides for her like I do- so I can talk her into this on most nights

After a while she becomes numb and it becomes routine
That's grooming 101 - now she's a part of my team

Working For The Crew

40

Gang-controlled sex trafficking is unique and complicated as it involves a culture of family. Just like the gang culture itself, as explained in the gang portion of this curriculum, the gang becomes the victim's family, and the words to live by are "family over everything." The gang becomes everything to the victim that family represents; love, loyalty, protection, and provision. This is why it becomes increasingly difficult to break the trauma bond as well as the loyalty the victim feels for the gang. The gang represents a story of escape for the victim; an escape from dysfunctional abusive/neglectful home, alcoholic parents, abuse, and neglect. It presents itself as an escape from the pain, the hurt, the memories and anything else the victim is trying to get away from. The gang promises the love and attention that isn't received at home. This particular culture of a family also makes it challenging for the victim to stay away from the gang even after being separated. To really understand the complexities of gang-controlled sexual exploitation you have to understand key concepts related to loyalty and family. The threats made by the gang also play a huge role. This is part of the "code of the streets."

Gang-controlled trafficking recruitment is similar to gang recruitment. It starts with friendly peer conversations, then associating with other gang members, sharing common interests, and slowly the gang life becomes conditioned. Whether it's gang-controlled trafficking or gang recruitment, a phenomenon has always been utilizing social media and the internet. Social media has made recruitment more accessible and quicker due to access to sensitive information and targeting the masses. Gangs prey upon the vulnerabilities of individuals to acquire compliance and meet their needs. Similar to pimp-controlled operations, gangs brand or mark victims showing allegiance to a specific gang.

Of the complicated parts of gang-controlled exploitation, it is important to understand gang culture. There is a system of rules, vocabulary, dances, hand signs, code, alphabets, and customs within specific groups. Gangs can have a hierarchy that exists to state the rules and regulations of the gang. In reality, this manifesto, bible, rulebook, states the laws to execute orders and ensure that the unit functions correctly. This is where the common phrases of "snitches get stitches" or "code of the street don't trust law enforcement" come from.

Gang-Controlled Sexual Exploitation Operations work differently and are considered to differentiate between two categories:

1. **Gang Motivated Sexual Exploitation Operations** refer to the process in which the gang is benefiting from the sexual exploitation. Specifically, more than one gang member is benefiting from the sale of a victim and the use of gang coercive tactics are used. These coercive tactics can include but are not limited to: glorifying the gang, threats of being harmed by the entire gang, or learning secrets such as gang dances, handshakes, reciting of rules, codes, manifestos, bibles, etc. Gang Motivated Sexual Exploitation has been seen with all types of gangs on a transnational, national and local/hybrid level.

2. **Gang Related Sexual Exploitation Operations** refer to the process in which one sole gang member is benefiting from the sexual exploitation. This is remarkably similar to a Pimp Controlled Operation as the gang member is attaining financial gain from the sale of the victim but also is using coercive tactics. Gang Related Sexual Exploitation is often seen with more national-based gangs or hybrid/local gangs.

Usually, the gang controlled sexual exploitation occurs by the leaders or dominant figures within the gang. The traffickers can work independently (gang related) or with other gang members (gang-motivated). The victims are often trafficked within the gang or by a sole gang member. Gang members have been known to set up sexual exploitation operations in trap houses, abandoned apartments, sheds, or buildings. They are mobile and transient and known to create business cards soliciting sex, have "skipping parties" for the purpose of soliciting sex or provide door to door services which includes having the victim knock on doors soliciting sex for money.

Gang-controlled commercial sexual exploitation enterprises exist and operate in the areas where they have claimed their territory. The victims of this exploitation often live in these neighborhoods or are brought in right after school. Gang-controlled operations service clientele who also live in these communities, for the apparent reason that they have more control in their familiar territories. Victims can be your everyday youth going to school on a regular basis and sleeping in their beds. It is an incredibly high-profit enterprise and low risk of prosecution.

I am asking you to think outside the box. Think about that five-year-old boy, abandoned by his family, growing up in abuse and residing in a gang-infested community. Every day he is told to go away and one day a friendly man covered in pretty colors befriends him. Gives him food because he hasn't eaten and welcomes him in. That five-year-old boy then starts hanging with these individuals and later learn they are a gang. He will learn sometime during his initiation process if he doesn't learn it earlier, that the gang is wrong or harmful, but by then that 5-year old boy will say its too late, not worth the change, or want to continue in the lifestyle. In the years I have worked with gang-involved youth, traumatic bonding has always been a common theme. Traumatic bonding is "strong emotional ties that develop between two persons where one person intermittently harasses, beats, threatens, abuses, or intimidates the other." (Dutton & Painter, 1981). My work with even some of the highest-ranking gang members depicts the level of trauma, pain, injury, and verbal and emotional abuse that they endured getting to the ranking that they are at.

My passion and focus initially began working with gang-involved youth. The complex nature of gang membership, rules, codes, mentality, recruitment, manifestos, graffiti, and tattoos was appealing and in all honesty, contributed to the development of my passion for victims of gang-controlled exploitation. Gang-controlled exploitation victims are often assumed and treated as if they are gang members. As if they are that thug that "chose" to hang with the bad boys. As if they only had substance abuse issues or presented antisocial traits and attitudes. As if they were sexually promiscuous and associated with the bad boys.

In the years I have been working with the population, I have only worked with females as it related to the gang-controlled exploitation. I believe that it is related to the bravado or machismo aspect of the gangs. Gangs are big wicked tough. When you think of gang members you do not think of the innocent individuals that are politely asking victims to give a blowjob for $20. You think of the big bad gang member that forces, demands, manipulates his way. Often gang members present with a misogynistic, macho and/or homophobic attitude. As a result, gang-controlled operations typically do not exploit minors for the gang's financial gain.

Loyalty is probably one of the most important concepts in the gang culture. Victims show an extreme amount of commitment because the gang has become their family. The connection and trauma bond are not only tied to one person; it is linked to the gang and all members. Often, gangs manipulate victims to recruit other victims. This is similar to the "Bottom Bitch" phenomenon (a tactic commonly used in the pimp culture where a woman is known as the top of the hierarchy of the females and receives the most trust and often most money). The following explains what I have termed *gang girl recruiters:*

AMERICAN DREAM

The American Dream is to go to school become educated to get a nice 9-5
But that's fiction to a lot of us and that's not where the reality lies
How you going to school when you're taking care of your baby sisters?
And your pregnant mother who's on her 3rd kid in 3 years and is about to deliver?

Where's daddy? Who the hell knows. Which one is my real dad? Depends on which way the wind blows.
So being like mama is really all a bitch knows.
But I'm not like the rest of these little hoes. See I'm the bottom bitch-
I'm the one that all the traffickers really know.
They love my physique they know that I'm sweet
That's why they send me to school these newbies to make them similar to me

Moving up this way is the way to my fame
They know my name and know I'm down until the end of the game

The head bitch in charge over all of these broads
Me and the bosses living large
I'm at the throne looking at these young bitches I own
Who all one day want to take my place on this throne

Way deep in this life and there's no turning back
If they need me to collect money or put on the mask, rob their stash- then I'm down for that
If somebody been running their lip and they need it smacked
If they need me to cut a chick quick because they were a rat- well I'm down for that!

I'm the most loyal one. I'm beneath no one. When we ride looking for possibilities, I'm the one riding shotgun
Live for the moment live for the fun
Bottom bitch and this is my family
Without them, I don't have anyone

Working For The Crew 46

The grooming process can be short or extensive depending on the victim. In most cases, once the victim is "chosen" by the gang, a gang member befriends her and becomes her 'boyfriend.' The gang will first try to sell 'the story' to the victim and then gain her love, affection, and loyalty. The 'boyfriend' acts as her savior and quickly gains her trust. She is introduced to drugs and alcohol to form a dependency. She may or may not be given nice things at first. As time goes on, the romance fades and she begins to be mistreated, disrespected, belittled, and abused. This is where she begins to dissociate and believe she is nothing more than property and a piece of garbage. The victim does not belong to one specific gang member. She belongs to all of them. Gang-controlled operations may also place brands on victims in the forms of markings or tattoos. They can be used to ensure ownership to others. It is a constant reminder of their slavery and acts as a key component in the dissociating process. The 'marking' examples can include a traditional brand with a hot object, a tattoo with the trafficker's name on it, the victim's 'new name,' some scar induced by cutting or carving on the skin.

UNDERSTANDING DEMAND

*As you continue to flip the page
One thing that's evident here and we want to make clear is that it is easily accessible and it doesn't matter about age
This isn't illegal- imagine if someone said u could still pay for slaves*

*Reasons why? Fantasies fulfilled - statistics show the deal
16% of men have paid for sex
For intimacy or to not have intimacy after sex
For the thrill or some type of pathology
A lot of men pay for it just for the variety*

*And ease at which it is to obtain
Type it in google click on pictures no need to exchange names
Other countries and it's similar to the same
Imagine going to a Starbucks one day
Pointing at and trying a lot of different cafes
Essentially substitute cafe for women and men and they are doing this the same way*

Except a lot of it's not voluntary done

I am always asked about the buyers. People always want to know what is being done about them. Who is addressing their issue? What can we do to a eradicate demand? The reality is there are amazing organizations directed to eliminating demand. Prevention needs to focus on demand as well as educating children and adolescents about an appropriate healthy sexual relationship or healthy relationships in general. I think I say the following to every parent and in every speaking engagement; We say to our kids that if someone is touching them they need report it. We often leave out that if you were touching someone else you need to tell us that as well and the issue must be addressed.

Several studies reveal that men who buy women in sexual exploitation come from all nationalities, races, and walks of life. In a U.S. study, the jobs of buyers purchasing sex ranged from the working class, such as fast food employees, truckers, oil rig and pipeline workers, or warehouse workers, to professional prominent community members, such as businessmen, lawyers, doctors, politicians, and dentists. The victims I have worked with over the years have been purchased by men ranging from 14 to men in their 90s.

In the aspects of buyers of gang-controlled sexual exploitation, the characteristics of these individuals are any age, race, males, and working. This often includes men providing for their families, good exterior lives, and looking to fulfill sexual interests. Their mentality shifts to; I need to achieve my deviant interest. Someone will be willing to be paid for this. I'm helping them by paying them for sex, sex is just sex.

It should be noted that regarding gangs, recruiting can occur at an early age. I have learned that the earlier a child has begun associating with gangs (before the age of ten), the likelihood of engagement in commercial sex increases. Those gang members that have been forced to associate with gangs since they were a child can be seen as having sex with females involved in commercial sex. Numerous gang involved youth I have worked with over the years have been forced or coerced to engage in sexual acts with "prostitutes."

Unfortunately, the horrific part about the demand-side of things is that the victims are not viewed as victims. They are viewed as more of a sexual interest than anything else.

It is that mentality that continues the drive the demand side of things.

Working For The Crew 51

AWAKENING AND UNDERSTANDING THE VICTIMS MINDSET

WHY DID THIS HAVE TO HAPPEN TO ME??!!!
Those are the words I screamed at the top of my lungs during therapy
Similar to the words I yell when I have flashbacks of PTSD
All of these emotions bottled inside of me

Sometimes I just sit and cry
Why would someone want to have sex with someone who is 5
Why?
I hated my insides
Because I felt like I was ruined before I was fully formed
And with all of this confusion a new found emotion was born

Anger
Anger at the world because you don't know what I have had to endure and because I did what?
What did I do to have this happen to me? Tell me what?
So I kept these emotions shut
Because it's all that I can control
I cry during regular checkups I hate annual physicals
Every time I see my body exposed
I grow cold

Why couldn't this have happened to you instead?
Why couldn't u be the one scared every night u lay in bed?

I see kids living the life I should have had and it makes me mad
I rob and sometimes steal because now people know how it feels to lose something they had
Seeing you experience the pain I felt makes me glad

All these diagnoses I've gotten through therapy
All these groups and medications they want to use to treat me

But I still cry wondering WHY DID THIS HAVE TO HAPPEN TO ME??!!!

PART 2

If you have gotten this far, you understand the above is indicative of Veronica's history of abuse. As a child, she had been abused, grown up with an understanding that the world is not safe had, uncomfortable feelings about herself, and overall felt different. A long time ago I heard someone say that sexual abuse is a "soul murder." At the time, I know I thought something sarcastic of "wow, that is dramatic." Looking back at it now, commercial sexual exploitation, a form of sexual abuse is a "soul murder." Its sole intention is to eliminate any safety, healthy appropriate boundaries and sexual behaviors and dramatically affect the development of one's self.

The overall perceptions and mindset of victims when encountering a gang member attempting to lure them into sexual exploitation is extreme vulnerability. The great myths that the gangs sell make victims believe in the sense of hope. Hope that whatever they were going through will be eliminated by associating with gang members. Hope that the gang will offer excitement. Hope that the gang can protect them. Hope that the gang is a new family. Hope that money can solve problems internally and externally. Hope that overall life will be better.

It is important to keep in mind that as there is no specific stereotype for victims of trafficking, there are also no warning signs that are consistent across the board. Changes in behavior, peer group and dress can be different depending on the pimp/trafficker and the specific victim. There is no standard empirically-based profile of warning signs.

Often gang members will begin to supply their victims with material items such as clothing or iPods, cell phones, etc. This is usually a part of the grooming process. The electronics also serve as a way for the gang-controlled trafficker to communicate with the victim. Unexplained cell phones can be huge indicators that something is going on as it raises the question of who could be paying for the cell phone service. Purchasing clothing articles for the victim can also be a strategy to get the victim to start dressing differently, such as in a more provocative way or to the trafficker's taste. There are common preconceived notions that victims of sexual exploitation wear fishnet stockings, high heels, and lots of makeup. This is not the case. Times have evolved and clothing is not a significant factor that it once was. Victims are dressing in everyday attire of jeans, a hoodie, and sneakers. Traffickers, victims, and buyers are substantially a lot more focused towards not rising attention to the operation.

Often when youth are exploited or victimized, personal changes will occur. They begin to associate with a different peer group as the trafficker attain more control. The gang will shift focus from the supports the victim knows to more gang members. They begin to associate with other youth and they can now identify the norms of the gang which include negative behaviors, perceptions, and thoughts. If the trafficker can isolate their victim from friends and family, they can then exert more force and control. In many cases the intent is to turn the victim against friends and family, making the trafficker the only person the victim will begin to depend on.

It should also be noted that changes in a peer group may not always occur. Traffickers often teach victims to not change their behavior and social structure to reduce suspicion. Often these victims become withdrawn from their families. They may become runaways, skip school (truancy), or begin to engage in high-risk behaviors including drug use. Drugs are an essential component of trafficking and are introduced almost immediately. This begins substance abuse dependency and allows them to begin exploiting the victim while he/she is under the influence, which reduces resistance.

To further illustrate the frequency of misdiagnoses and the importance of knowing the history and experience of each client, the following poem illustrates the need to focus on individual planning and awareness of knowledge of trauma and trafficking. The shift of the focus when addressing, interacting, communicating and treating these victims, must include *The Life. The Life* in which the gang wants them to know. ....*The Life* of gang banging. *The Life* of commercial sex.

We are in love.

I will change my name for you.
I will give you my old identity including my driver's license.
I have rehearsed my story if anyone asks.
I will give you all the money I make.
I will make what you tell me I must make.

I accept my beating if I fail to make enough.

I am protecting my family.
Therefore, I continue.

I will call you by whatever name you want. You are my everything.
I get sick from disease and germs of the strangers I have sex with.

I want your love and will work hard for your attention.
You are my world.

I will never betray you. EVER.

MENTAL HEALTH AND TREATMENT NEEDS

A series of difficulties often arise when working with and identifying victims of gang-controlled sexual exploitation. In many cases, these complications can hinder the proper identification of victims. Below are some of the most common difficulties and misconceptions.

Not Identifying as victims

Typically, victims of sexual exploitation do not identify themselves as victims. This is attributed to the grooming and manipulation enforced by the offender. Often, they are seduced into a romantic relationship and are conditioned to believe that all of this is part of the relationship and that they have to do these things if they truly 'love' their 'boyfriend' (who in reality is the trafficker). Another scenario is that of a victim who is trying to convince him/herself that they are in control and 'choose' this life. Ultimately, the most reliable silencer is the fear inflicted by the trafficker if they were to ever speak of their exploitation.

Survival Sex

This has been a topic of debate for a great deal of time and can have many different underlying perceptions. Survival sex can describe the practice of people who are homeless exchanging sex for food, a place to sleep, for drugs or other basic needs. There are some believers that believe survival sex is a job, a form of acting out, etc.

Often, victims of sexual exploitation are seen as willing participants because they want to do this to survive. What is the definition of their survival and to what extent should a person have to endure rape, abuse and other traumas for 'survival?' What are the specific circumstances of that particular person and are they really doing this to survive? It has already been determined that force, fear, and coercion are three main elements in trafficking. These are also three elements that abolish free will and choice.

It is also important to note that runaways are the most targeted population and traffickers take advantage of this vulnerability. If in fact a minor is forced to engage in a sexual act in exchange for food, shelter or basic needs, he or she is being exploited and this situation is a classic example of Domestic Minor Sex Trafficking.

Sexual abuse is not a motivation for prostitution. It is a trauma that breaks down a human being's self-worth and humanity. This makes them an easy target as they may have already lost their sense of self-worth, making them extremely vulnerable and naive.

A key concept to Gang-Controlled Exploitation relates to the loyalty to the trafficker. Victims are typically indoctrinated into the victimization of being exploited, which contributes to the loyalty to the offender. The victims become fearful of what would happen to their trafficker if they disclose. They now have a trauma bond and an extreme loyalty, which blinds them to their reality. For some service and treatment providers this can become confusing, especially if the concept of loyalty isn't understood. The victim will deny ever being harmed by the trafficker and even talk about all the good deeds they witnessed their trafficker do. They will talk about how well they were treated and how they were taken care of. They insist that this person would never harm them.

Typically with gang members and individuals involved with gang-controlled exploitation, victims are told not to talk to outsiders. This includes case managers, law enforcement, and therapists. More specifically, the "code of the street" is the concept that if you speak out against the gang, or if you disclose anything about what you've seen or what they've done to you, they will come after you to either hurt or kill you or your loved ones. This concept is known as "snitching," and the code is that "snitches get stitches." These threats induce a large amount of fear in their victims, which aids in their ability to control them and keep them in the life.

Looking through a trauma informed clinical lens, Veronica portrays the victim's mindset during the horrific offense. This is the victim who likely has sustained and carries with her layer upon layer of beatings, mind control, rape, drugs, told when and what she can eat, where and when she can sleep. She has been diminished and devalued with much of her personhood left in tatters. While at first glance and on the surface, the clinical picture of many of the Gang-Controlled Exploitation Victims are Oppositional Defiant Disorder, Conduct Disorder, or Borderline Personality Disorder. The truth is that many of these adolescent victims suffer from a syndrome called Complex Post Traumatic Stress Disorder, a term that is not officially recognized in the DSM but is commonly used by the experts in the field of trauma, i.e. Van der Kolk, Herman, Levine and others.

As Judith Herman describes it, "survivors of prolonged abuse develop characteristic personality changes, including deformations of relatedness and identity" (Ford, 2015). It should be clear, often at the point of these victims interaction with law enforcement, social services, and court services, that many of the symptoms of Complex PTSD may overlap or co-occur with symptoms of other mental disorders such as opposition, conduct, or substance abuse related disorders. A complicating factor is the consideration that many of these victims may indeed have had pre-existing disorders even before entering the life. This renders them even more vulnerable to the brutality of their life on the street. Certainly, many of them present with significant depression, somatization, acting out/defiant behaviors, anxiety, and hypervigilance, a state of constant stress arousal scanning the environment for danger. The opposite, numbing through dissociation, may also be present, as well as substance problems that will need to be teased out and treated. Many females may have been escaping from homes where they were physically or sexually abused. Therefore, they may have even deeper trust issues and a more desperate sense of hopelessness about starting out in life as they have already learned the tragic truth that they were abused by the very caretakers who they believed they could trust.

The victim often struggles to acknowledge deter association with gangs. They are ashamed, have been told and feel they will never amount to anything, and think this life is better than what they went through. The excitement outweighs consequences, feeling trapped, afraid to leave, fear of retaliation, and they fear the change of what "normalcy" is. There is a considerable correlation between domestic violence and sexual exploitation. Victims are stuck in the power and control dynamics, feeling that if they leave something worse may occur.

As a result of those reasons, gang-controlled sexual exploitation victims do not seek help and they continue to be abused. They are often normalizing the abuse or unwilling/conditioned to think being a victim is weak. Particularly, gang involved youth at high risk or those who have been sexually exploited may be highly resistant to the process of speaking with adults about life experiences. They are fearful for their own safety and may be highly protective of any relationship, particularly one with the person(s) grooming or exploiting them. Unlike traditional clients who are seeking treatment for symptoms related to trauma, these youth are often highly guarded emotionally, resistant to treatment as he/she may not perceive themselves as needing help and are highly aversive to any physical or emotional vulnerability. These youth may also fear for their lives if thought to be "cooperating" with adults considered "at risk for talking with law enforcement" by gang members.

Few professionals possess the skill and competency to work with victims of gang-controlled exploitation as it is a different approach than theoretically used. Working with this population means to not only be aware of gang dynamics and sexual exploitation, but understanding complex trauma. These are the victims that will tell you multiple times to never come back. The ones that will tell you "you are here for a paycheck," the ones that are resistant, aggressive, and repeatedly may say they don't want the help and that things will never get better.

While the concept of collaboration is universally understood in private practice, community settings, treatment facilities, private and public government sectors, and businesses, in real time, it doesn't always happen. Professionals sometimes guard their domains and keep relevant information to themselves. Hospitals often leave out vital information in discharge referrals. Private practitioners sometimes hold themselves apart from community agencies and even within treatment programs, critical information is inadvertently left out of interagency communications and/or staff meetings. While this is never an effective way to provide continuity of care, in this particular population continuity of care takes on a whole new meaning.

These children and adolescents have lived months or years, maybe their entire lives, experiencing intermittent abuse and serial abandonment. As a result, they come into any system or program immersed in suspicion and trusting no one. It then becomes imperative for all involved to be trauma-informed, trained in working with the special needs of this population, and insuring that comprehensive histories, diagnoses, and treatment plans are shared with everyone who is to be involved with this client. For anything to fall through the cracks means substantially adding to the risk that this person will leave treatment and return to what is familiar. While that is always a risk, it is not up to us to help them on their way back. Constant communication with ALL sources including treatment providers, law enforcement, social services, probation, placing agency, and family is essential to effectively manage and meet the needs of your client. This ensures that all appropriate services are put in place and that all necessary safety measures are put in place as well.

From an agency, corporation, government, business sector, for-profit, non-profit or whatever the affiliation, standard procedures must be in place. Collaboration means addressing the issue as it relates to gang-controlled sexual exploitation or sexual exploitation in general. It means not trying to brush it under the rug. It means acknowledging ONE victim if not the actual amount. It means hiring people to be "experts" and to educate others. If the plan is to become active and involved with this population, is your job to become the "expert" regarding this population.

CASE STUDY

Maria is a 16-year-old Hispanic young lady who lives with her mom and two younger brothers, ages 12 and 10. Maria's mother has resided in the U.S. for ten years, but is undocumented. She migrated from El Salvador via Border Coyotes. Maria was not born in the US; however, her brothers were.

Maria came to the attention of Juvenile Court due to truancy and repeated runaways. Her mother stated in court that she did not know how to control her and as a result, she was referred to CPS. The family was assigned a prevention worker who began working with the family to secure stabilized housing and treatment services for Maria. Services were short lived as Maria ran away again. The mother reported that she believed that Maria was not only gang involved, but was prostituting. Later, it was verified that Maria was being trafficked by this gang.

Maria was picked up by police and placed at a local youth shelter. The police made several visits to the shelter and contacted the prevention worker to report that Maria was in danger and should be moved from the shelter. At the same time, the Department of Homeland Security contacted the prevention worker to verify that a legitimate "Green Light" had been issued on Maria and she needed a secure placement.

Maria did not meet the criteria for a locked residential facility or for detention. Numerous staff began searching for a safe and secure place for Maria. Since no placement was located, the worker took the case to court. During the court proceeding, it was stated that Maria's gang involved "boyfriend" contacted the mother asking very personal questions. This included information about the prevention worker such as her address, names of children, and type of car. Based on this information, the Judge placed Maria in a secure setting for a brief period of time.

Unfortunately, this story does not have a happy ending. Maria continues to be trafficked and abused by the gang. This story began the collaborative process.

Multiple agencies were involved in this case and no one liked the outcome. Everyone involved agreed to meet to debrief what had occurred in this case. The result of the meeting was the realization that everyone had a piece of the story and no one had the full story. Law enforcement identified that there are many Maria's out there and something needed to be done.

Since no specific data on this population was available, youth in detention and the youth shelter were reviewed for risk factors such as multiple runaways, truancy, gang affiliation, etc. This was done in an informal manner. Lists were compiled, and workers were asked to identify those youth suspected of being involved with trafficking. The list grew to the hundreds and the participating agencies recognized the community had a problem.

It was agreed that the initial meeting would occur and in a brief period of time a policy group and a multidisciplinary case review team were established. As a result, multiple youth were identified that currently were runaways and because of a multi-jurisdictional effort multiple youth were picked up and provided treatment services.

SEX MINOR TRAFFICKING AS A CHILD WELFARE ISSUE

If there is a single theme to this year's Trafficking in Persons (TIP) Report, it is the conviction that there is nothing inevitable about trafficking in human beings. That conviction is where the process of change really begins- with the realization that just because a certain abuse has taken place in the past doesn't mean that we have to tolerate that abuse in the future or that we can afford to avert our eyes. Instead, we should be asking ourselves-what if that victim of trafficking was my daughter, son, sister, or brother...ending modern day slavery isn't just a fight we should attempt-it is a fight we can and must win."-John F. Kerry, Secretary of State (Kerry, 2016).

Sex trafficking of minors in the United States encompasses a widespread criminal enterprise, the presence of which has been documented in all 50 states. Human trafficking is a form of modern-day slavery. (Human Trafficking of children in the United States, n.d.). With the passage of the Trafficking Victims Protection Act (TVPA) in 2000, sex trafficking is recognized as a crime. According to the TVPA, any minor under the age of 18 who is involved in a commercial sex act is a victim of human Trafficking (TVPA, 2000). When the crime involves a minor, this crime does not require proof of force, fraud, or coercion. This includes sex in exchange for anything of value given to any person, including trafficking of a minor by a family member for rent or drugs, a minor trading a sex act for shelter, food, a ride, etc., prostitution of a minor by a pimp, gang or gang member(s), or pornography where the minor is provided something of value to perform sex acts on camera or video (TVPA, 2000).

As discussed in the Chapter on Collaboration, the U.S. Department of justice estimates that approximately 450,000 children run away from home each year in this country. Field experts believe that a significant majority of youth that run away or are throwaways, kicked out of their home by parents, become involved in some form of sexual exploitation within 48 hours of leaving home. 33% of those youth are exploited in sex trafficking within 48 hours (Allen, 2010) Experts state that it is not a matter of "if" a youth is exposed to sexual exploitation within four nights on the streets, but a certainty.

Another significant trend is that many States have redefined trafficking victimization as child sexual abuse. This moves the focus away from Juvenile Justice and into the Child Welfare arena. Often victims of trafficking are made known to the "system" as a result of petty, status offense crimes. More and more states, in an effort to meet the requirements of the TVPA are waiving the traditional requirement of Child Protective Services that they are not able to investigate child abuse unless the alleged perpetrator is in a caretaker role. New laws and interpretation of current laws are redefining the role of a pimp or gang member exploiting a minor as in a "caretaker" role, thus meeting the Child Protective mandate for intervention. This shift creates a tsunami of increased opportunity for treatment and services for victims. While Juvenile Justice must continue to hold victims accountable for serious felony crimes, victims are no longer labeled as "prostitutes" and are seen as the child sex abuse victims that they are. Research has shown that the most beneficial approach to addressing the needs of trafficking victims is a multidisciplinary approach. (See Collaboration Chapter).

Another important issue is that youth who are or have been in the foster care system are particularly vulnerable to exploitation. The FBI reports that 60% of child sex trafficking victims recovered through FBI raids across the U.S. in 2013 were from foster homes or group homes, (Foster Care Youth Institute/Sex Trafficking). Foster care youth are especially vulnerable because of past history of abuse, history of needing to adjust to frequent moves and others having control of their lives including obtaining basic needs. A foster care system that all too often has difficulty providing the intense trauma treatment youth need increases the vulnerability.

The shift in definition of minor sexual exploitation from juvenile justice to child welfare and the significantly high numbers of youth involved in foster care exploited by traffickers brings to focus training and intervention efforts on Child Welfare staff. What could the impact be?

With high caseloads already stressing both Child Protective Services and Foster Care systems across the U.S., many are concerned that introducing minors into the Child Welfare system, particularly through CPS complaints will break the system at it's core. Yes, high caseloads are an issue, but what often frustrates workers is the inability to make the "right thing happen" for a youth, whatever that may be. A collaborative process between child welfare agencies and other child serving agencies eases the burden of everyone involved but does pose some additional challenges for helping professionals who are providing direct service treatment.

In an effort to assist you in understanding how to best navigate a complex system such as child welfare and a collaborative team of professionals from multiple agencies, it may be helpful to understand the responsibilities and mandates of these entities as well as learn how to best assist child welfare and other agencies staff most effectively.

Child Protective Services

Every State and jurisdiction in the United States has a law mandating the activities of Child Protective Services. Each State may have slight variations and specific rules, but in general, Child Protective Services (CPS) is mandated to investigate valid complaints of abuse and/or neglect and to preserve a family unit whenever possible. Most States differentiate CPS from Law Enforcement activities based upon the role of the alleged abuser. CPS is most often designated to investigate valid complaints if the alleged abuser is in a caretaker role with the child. This can include a parent(s), babysitter, relative, teacher, coach etc. The work of CPS is considered a "Civil" action in Court. This means that the focus of the investigation that CPS completes is to determine if a child has been abused and how to best keep a child safe. If abuse is determined to have occurred, the case is processed in a Civil court meaning the court is focused on determining if there is sufficient evidence that a "Finding" can be made, prompting further CPS action under the guidance of the Court. This is why CPS workers are the professionals that remove a child from an unsafe family. Law Enforcement is most focused on investigations in the circumstances of a criminal act. A stranger, someone not in a caretaker role who abuses a child is charged criminally and it is considered a "Criminal" action in Court and the expectation is that a person will be found guilty or not guilty and punished criminally if found guilty. Often CPS and Law

Enforcement are investigating cases at the same time. CPS is investigating if a child is safe and Law Enforcement is investigating if the crime of child abuse has occurred. It always works better when CPS and Law Enforcement work together. (See Collaboration Chapter)

Child Advocacy Centers (CAC) serve as a way for CPS and Law Enforcement to work together and to share information. A CAC provides a child friendly, neutral environment that allows both Law Enforcement and CPS to share information regarding a child interview so that the child or youth only has to tell their story once. CAC records and/or tapes the interview so it can also be used in Court proceedings. Many CAC's also serve as a "one stop shop" for victims to be able to have medical examinations and other investigative procedures in a safe environment. Most importantly the child only has to participate in the investigative process one time.

CPS is also mandated to conduct "Family Assessments". This is a way to assess if a child is safe in a home or other environment when the crime of child abuse may not be present or able to be proven. An example of when a Family Assessment may take place is in the case of a child living in a home where there is a suspicion of neglect due to extreme poverty or lack of skilled parenting. Not a crime per se, but the family may require intervention to be able to keep a child safe, healthy and thriving. If a family needs additional support or monitoring to ensure safety, the family may be referred for services through the portion of the CPS unit called "On-going CPS Services". Some jurisdictions seek private providers to perform these services.

The focus of a CPS unit should be on child safety rather than on convicting a criminal. Historically, when a youth was found to be engaging in sexual activities involving money and a "buyer", this was investigated by Law Enforcement. The youth was often treated as if he/she were engaged in voluntary prostitution. Charges could be filed and the youth could be sent into the Juvenile Justice system, placed on probation or even incarcerated. The TPVA prevents this approach by clearly identifying sexual exploitation of a minor to be exploitation not prostitution. The minor is not held responsible for the actions of a trafficker.

Foster Care and Adoption

If a child or youth is determined to be at risk of harm in the family home, every effort must be made by CPS to provide services to the family to remediate the problem. Most often, there are effective interventions that can prevent a child from having to enter foster care. In extreme cases, the situation may be so potentially risky or acutely harmful to the children in a home that CPS will have to make the decision to remove that child and place him or her into Foster Care. These actions are made under tight oversight by the Court. There are times when CPS may petition the Court to remove a child and the Court rules that the child remain in the home. This occurs if there is not enough direct evidence to demonstrate risk or harm. Judges know that placement of a child into foster care causes trauma even when it is absolutely appropriate. Therefore, they are very cautious about situations that are ambiguous. This can be especially challenging in cases of trafficking. Without direct cause and effect indicating a parent has overtly trafficked a youth, a Judge may challenge an attempt to remove, even when the CPS worker is concerned about a parent's willingness to protect. This is important to know when working with CPS as workers are not always able to make the decisions they would prefer.

Once CPS determines placement into Foster Care is necessary, the child or youth is placed in a foster home or a temporary placement. Foster Care workers work very hard to make sure that a youth does not need to move more than two times, however the reality is that finding foster homes willing to take on the challenges of trafficked youth are extremely limited. Often youth are placed into a youth shelter or group home situation upon removal. This is problematic from a safety and therapeutic perspective. Trafficked youth are often uncooperative with a placement, preferring to remain with their trafficker. Trauma bonds with traffickers are extremely strong and safety is an active concern with these youths. Trafficking youth may be accustomed to having access to drugs, truancy from school and a lifestyle that affords them adult status albeit abusive. When a youth is non-compliant with a placement and running away is a risk, a youth may be placed in a residential setting with more structure and often locked doors. While the adults responsible for the youth feel more relaxed that the youth is safe, the residential treatment setting, while temporarily necessary, may be counter-indicated therapeutically.

Another important issue to note about youth in child welfare is that the moment the young person is placed into Foster care, the goal shifts to finding a permanent placement. Foster care workers must file a goal with the court. A return home goal is typically a preferred goal. Even in situations in which a parent has been abusive or neglectful, the goal is initially for the youth to return home. This is because foster care workers are mandated to attempt to provide services to the family to promote potential reunification. Only in the most egregious situations is the goal to terminate parental rights. Every effort must be made to reunite a family whenever possible. This is often very challenging in situations of trafficked youth. As discussed throughout this book, youth who have been involved in trafficking form trauma bonds with their trafficker. Depending on the stage of the grooming process, a youth may believe the trafficker loves them and wishes to share the dream of having a "happy ever after" permanent family. Parents may be unable or unwilling to deal with the behavior presented by the youth who wishes to return to the trafficker.

These circumstances present a difficult double bind for foster care workers. How do you measure safety? Does a youth need to be locked against her will because she loves someone everyone else despises? Is the risk of running away sufficient to lock someone up against her will? Since we know that youth are best treated in the community, at what cost do we send her to a residential facility? On the other hand, what if the trafficker attempts to harm the youth, or the youth's family? What if the parents are unwilling to have her live at home because of risk to other children in the family? These are the questions that foster care workers must consider when seeking a placement and are endless and cause significant stress for the worker and the child welfare system as a whole.

Foster Care workers are charged with the role of caring for children and youth in the absence of the parent. They must ensure safety at all costs, making any risk significant. This has very real impact on the type of decisions workers make about youth who have been trafficked. The tolerance for any risk of future harm is very low. While it may make perfect therapeutic sense for a youth to remain in the community as the best option for future growth and recovery, the foster care worker is likely to recommend an option that removes the youth from the community. This is as a result of weighing the consequences of running away to the trafficker, drug use, safety issues regarding repercussions from traffickers etc.

When working with Child Welfare engaged youth and staff, it is important to remember is that so much is mandated that a worker may not be able to make decisions that appear to be obvious. When working with Child Welfare staff, communication is key and if you have a question, be sure to ask, seek information and make sure you understand the complex environment the worker is navigating. Always follow-up, with a worker each and every time you need to. Even if the worker does not respond, it is always helpful for the worker to receive as much information as possible.

A multidisciplinary team approach is very helpful with foster care youth. The Team can work together to develop the best possible plan to support the youth's needs. This may support youth to remain at home or in the community in a foster home if a team of professionals can add support. The foster care worker is working with the back up of the Team, which eases the burden from one person having sole responsibility.

COLLABORATION AND A MULTIDISCIPLINARY APPROACH

The Importance of Data
Do you think your community has a sex trafficking problem? If you believe your community has a problem, chances are it does. Sex trafficking of minors in the United States encompasses a widespread criminal enterprise, the presence of which has been documented in all 50 states. Additionally, law enforcement agencies in over 35 states and U.S. Territories have reported cases of sex trafficking within gang enterprises (National Gang Intelligence Center, 2001). Research suggests the occurrence of this atrocity is significantly under-reported yet the rise in reported and suspected incidence has been steadily increasing over recent years (Finklea, 2015). The U.S. Department of Justice estimates that approximately 450,000 children run away from home each year in this country. Field experts estimate that 33 percent of teen runaways and throwaways become involved in prostitution within 48 hours of leaving home (Allen, 2010). A case study completed in Virginia found that "Juveniles with increased vulnerability for trafficking, such as chronic runaways, homeless minors, and juvenile delinquents were not being identified as youth with a high risk of victimization through domestic minor sex trafficking" (Shared Hope, 2011). These youths were being misidentified and labeled with status offenses or as a child in Need of Services (CHINS).

Do you have data to support this claim? If not, is there data in your community that could help substantiate this idea? Data to support the claim that sex trafficking is occurring can come from many sources. However, unless a program or service is specifically related to sex trafficking, data will not be listed as such. To find quantitative data to support the occurrence of sex trafficking, many data elements may need to be examined and correlated to find patterns that lead to the conclusion that sex trafficking is occurring and perhaps, to what extent. Each discipline especially if state mandated, has a plethora of data and information that could be helpful. For example, Social

Services will have data on youth in foster care, how many times these youths leave their placements, etc. Child protective services will have data on abuse/neglect complaints and ongoing data regarding youth on their caseloads. The public school will have data on truancy. The Juvenile Court Services unit will have data on petitions and intake information related to status offenses like running away. Local law enforcement and or detention will have information directly related to gang involvement. At the end of this chapter, a case study will be presented that provides insight on specific data elements, and when placed together can begin to tell the story of the community.

Going forward, determine what data you want to track. Develop a spreadsheet that incorporates all the data and determine who is responsible for the collection.

What do I do now?
It has been determined that your community has a sex trafficking problem. What happens now? Who is responsible for identifying potential victims? Who is responsible for making sure this population is served appropriately? Who is in charge? If your community is like most in the country, the current system and infrastructure for addressing sex trafficking is disjointed and lacks a comprehensive approach. To best serve this population, research shows that the development and implementation of a cohesive and comprehensive multi-disciplinary system of care which approaches the issue of minor sex trafficking holistically will produce the best outcomes. Does your community have a team? Do you need to create a new team? How hard can it be to get a representative from all disciplines together in the same room to create a collaborative group that speaks with one voice?

The answer it can be a daunting task, but it can be done.

If the community has a Child Advocacy Center (CAC), a multidisciplinary team most likely already exists in the community. It is recommended to use the experience of this team or the team leaders as they can likely provide valuable experience in a successful team building process. If no CAC exists, however, it can still be done by following these steps.

Step one: Find a champion that is willing to make the initial contact to coordinate the meeting. It does not matter what agency the person comes from. If the process is done well, the outcome will be the same regardless of who called the first meeting. The person calling the meeting should be someone who has decision making capabiliities for their agency. Best case scenario is a middle manager or someone in a leadership role, but not necessarily executive leadership. Executives have full agendas and are not typically as tuned into the challenges of working with this population. You will want a champion who is willing to give up "turf issues" and mediate a cohesive group that can develop one vision and mission. The beginnings of a group start with the convener contacting his or her peers from varying agencies. Contacting those in which you already have an established relationship will make this process easier. Very little replaces a personal meeting to gain support and to have the opportunity to actively listen to concerns, perspectives and ideas. It is very important to have the right people at the table. It is recommended that each of the following agencies be represented at the first meeting:

- Child Welfare Staff (Child Protective Services and or Foster Care)
- Juvenile Court Services
- Local law enforcement to include counties and any towns included in the geographic area
- Federal law enforcement (FBI, Homeland Security)
- State or County Commonwealth Attorney's Office
- County Attorney's Office
- Victim Witness Programs
- Mental Health
- Health Department
- County School System
- Advocacy Groups
- Specialty treatment providers
- Forensic medical personnel
- Child Advocacy Center, if available

Expect that everyone in the room is not likely to have the same information regarding the issues facing your locality, the scope of trafficking in your community, or to have similar views on the root of the issue or the impact on victims. For example, the Juvenile Justice or Law Enforcement perspective may focus on the willingness of victims to participate in parties, substance use or even sexual activities. Child Welfare or Mental Health may be viewing through the trauma lens and may focus on the impact of the victims and surmise that only the traffickers are to blame. Others may deny a problem exists. Some may believe this is only an issue that targets one particular segment or group within the population. It is almost always politically unpopular to address this issue in a community...until there is a crisis.

Helping the initial group find a common vision may have to start very small, such as averting a crisis or prevention activities to avoid the issue from impacting the community. One common goal that is easier to embrace from many differing perspectives is to do whatever can be done to avoid a murder or bad press. Taking a proactive approach is always better than getting blindsided. Using data from the community research you have done and looking at data from neighboring jurisdictions or similar communities can be very helpful. Identifying unique qualifiers such as "we have an international airport" or "the Interstate goes right through our community" can help those who may be feeling protective of the community image and may provide a pathway to view information more openly.

No matter the issue, what is critical in this early stage for collaboration is to honor and respect all views in the room. Getting agreement on basic principles is helpful. For example, if there is disagreement regarding the scope of the issue, perhaps the group can agree that everyone in the room is committed to making sure trafficking does not impact the youth in the community, regardless of the differing opinions of the current numbers.

It is also vitally important to be openly respectful of every discipline's role, responsibility and mandates in the room. Despite a legal system that is fraught with built in conflict, everyone has a job to do, is committed to doing that job and is important in addressing the trafficking issue. Find common ground whenever possible. It may sound like a cliché, but focus on coming from a position of love, respect and openness to learning. If the team gets bogged down on the motivations of the victim's behaviors, the project will stall out quickly. If you cannot get everyone at the first meeting, that is ok. Continue to pursue those missing so they can be added to the team.

Another tool and approach that can be used to prepare for the first meeting is to send a simple survey to several agencies such as Court Services, Social Services, Juvenile Detention, law enforcement and any service providers that may have a perspective on this issue including prevalence in the community. This information can be the kick-off discussion at the first meeting.

Step Two: Set a time and place for a first meeting to happen. The goal of the first meeting is to discuss the topic of sex trafficking, to include any Federal or State legislation or mandates impacting your community as well as best practices that support the idea that this topic is best approached from a collaborative and multidisciplinary framework. Discuss the impact of trafficking on the community and if a survey was done, share the results and talk about them. Lastly, begin the dialogue regarding how the group wants to approach the subject and if the group wants to approach the subject. It is very important to discuss how often the group will meet and set the next meeting date, time and location. Do not wait too long to have the next meeting. After the meeting adjourns, make sure notes are compiled and sent out to the group members. This gives everyone the opportunity to process what occurred at the meeting and perhaps develop ideas of additional information that needs to be shared.

The convener of the group will want to make a personal contact with each member to gain feedback, opinions and to learn of any unspoken disagreements or concerns. Each member is vital to the process and every effort should be made to provide a platform for open and brutally honest feedback.

Several of the agencies represented on the team, may already have working relationships. For example, law enforcement and child protective services, in many localities, work closely together when investigating serious complaints of abuse or neglect. Mental Health staff may work closely with school personnel when a student is in crisis. It is important to make sure that all team members have the opportunity to talk at each meeting and that the group develops a way to reach consensus on difficult topics. Chatter outside of the room after meetings can sometimes derail the process. At one of the first meetings, it is helpful if each agency presents a brief presentation to discuss what their agency does, legal and agency mandates, and any barriers that could impact service delivery. These presentations can help explain the conflicts that can occur between the involved agencies. A breakdown in respect for the important role each member brings to the process results in an ineffective team. If one member is missing from the process, it should be identified as an incomplete team.

It takes time and energy to develop a cohesive team. A good facilitator for the group will enhance the group process and ensure that the group continues to move forward.
Step Three: Develop a structure that will assist in getting the work done.

For the most cohesive team, it is important for team members to develop a set of core values, principles, and protocols for all aspects of the project. Emphasis is placed on the importance of true teamwork, trust, partnership, and cooperation between all members of the group. It is recommended that a memorandum of understanding as well as a guiding philosophy be developed and signed by each agency represented at the table. In best practice areas, two teams are developed. These teams are divided by function. One team will provide oversight and develop policy related to trafficking while the other team focuses on specific cases and make recommendations. Once the project mission and value statements are solidified, specific protocols should be developed for each team so that all members understand who does what. Items to discuss include; who is facilitating each meeting, who takes notes, how often to meet, where and when, and the process for each meeting including agenda development.

It is helpful for a team to engage in a strategic planning process to gain direction and to benchmark goals and timelines. The Strategic Plan may evolve and shift over time as the trafficking business does, but having a vision and plan to get there assists all participating agencies to gain buy-in from agency leadership and justify the time, effort and financial investment necessary to seriously address this issue that can infest itself into a community so quickly.
There are numerous examples of communities that have made significant progress in a collaborative multi-disciplinary approach to trafficking. There are big scale projects such as the State of Florida's

statewide approach, geographical approaches such as in Walla Walla, Washington or more local programs such as the Child Advocacy (SEEN) project in the Suffolk County, Boston, Massachusetts approach. Each of these projects have been at the forefront of establishing best practice approaches that communities can take to confront and more successfully mediate the impact of trafficking within a community.

Best practice Teams regardless of size have some common themes and goals. Best practice Teams seek to:

-Establish a cohesive, multi-agency approach to the issue of trafficking;

-Address trafficking from a multi-phased approach that includes Prevention;

-Establish a comprehensive and cohesive community protocol to assess victim needs, address safety and medical issues and to provide basic care and treatment services to victims in a timely manner;

-Establish a comprehensive approach to legal issues that reduce impact and burden upon victims;

-Develop a comprehensive approach to legal and treatment needs of buyers.

The goal of a multidisciplinary approach is twofold. The Advisory Team focuses on policy issues, the goals and objectives of the approach and "big picture ideas" as discussed above. After this initial work is completed, another multidisciplinary team should be formed for the purpose of individual case review.

The Individual Case Review Team (ICR team) is charged with the responsibility of addressing victim needs with specific cases. This is the team that does the grassroots work to ensure that victims have access to services, monitors the progress of victims through the legal process and focuses on advocacy for the victim. Members of the Individual Case Review Team should include front line personnel from every agency represented on the Advisory Team. For example, the CPS Director may serve on the Advisory Team but the CPS workers assigned to trafficking cases will serve on the Individual Case Review Team. The Division Lead in Law Enforcement may serve on the Advisory Team but the actual officers and detectives who work with trafficking cases in the field will serve on the Individual Case Review Team. Each agency is represented on both the Advisory Team and the Individual Case Review Team.

The Individual Case Review Team meets when a trafficking victim has been brought to the attention of Child Protective Services, Law Enforcement, Juvenile Justice or any other portal of entry into the "system". The group is expected to share ideas, perspectives and concerns openly. The Individual Case Review Team should work collaboratively together under a Memorandum of Understanding that allows complete transparency and trust among each discipline. This is very similar to how a Child Advocacy Center Multi-Disciplinary Team works. Law Enforcement must be willing to listen to the opinion of Child Protective Services workers regarding the impact of victim trauma on the case. This could impact how Law Enforcement proceeds with a criminal investigation. At the same time, Child Protective Services workers must also be willing to listen to the legal implications for victims who have committed crimes. The decision to move forward with charges for example, is complex in these cases. Some may feel that because of the nature of the trauma a victim experiences at the hands of the trafficker (threats, beatings, manipulation) that the victim should be immune from accountability for crimes committed in the name of the gang. At the same time, there may be other Team members who feel passionately that victims should be held accountable for major crimes committed despite the circumstances.

The challenge of working through the above example is significant and should be actively addressed by the group facilitator. It can take years for a fully functional multi-disciplinary team to see a case from the same lens. Extensive training, team building exercises, and group discussion is critical, however, building mutual respect for the role of each discipline is key. Honoring each discipline equally is critical. Law Enforcement may view social service workers as "thug huggers." Social services should feel free to wear that distinction with pride and honor. At the same time social services workers may view Law Enforcement as negative or too tough with the rules. Law Enforcement should feel free to remind social service workers that they are the ones who are going to experience gunfire in the field to protect them if ever necessary. Humor is an excellent tool to honor, acknowledge and support differences. While team members who can gently and respectfully use humor to voice challenges, absolute respect must be given at all times to each team member's viewpoint as a representative of their own discipline. The Team should be clear about legal protocols, boundaries, roles and responsibilities, and seek to honor all of these in the case of decision making. This can be highly challenging because these issues conflict and are often directly opposed. As a group, best practices should be established that support the mandates of each discipline. Training together is a good way to learn to anticipate what some of these opposing issues may be. Learning how other Teams across the country have successfully addressed them can me very helpful.

There are few professional activities that are more difficult than serving on a multi-disciplinary team, yet none are as rewarding for the professionals involved or for the clients served. This is absolutely true in trafficking cases. The truth is that these cases rarely surface in a smooth and routine manor. Cases surface in the middle of the night, the street officers may not always know the best responses, housing is often a significant challenge, safety is hard to ensure and victims are not often cooperative.

This is a good time to read the chapter on Compassion Fatigue...

COMPASSION, FATIGUE, BURNOUT AND SECONDARY TRAUMATIC STRESS

The Truth
Working with victims of exploitation can be very rewarding. Having the honor and influence in potentially saving a life or numerous lives requires a higher calling to service. When law enforcement activities are finished, and the drama of the moment subsides, there stand those tasked with helping a victim begin to put the pieces of a shattered life together. The helping professional is left holding the pieces, often begging the victim to at least try to see another day. This can be heart wrenching, gut busting, soul wounding work. Victims often don't want your help. They agitate you, they rip you off emotionally and at times swipe your stuff. They promise with all their hearts to do something yet seconds later do the opposite.

As the helper, you are the giver in the relationship. The victim is the taker. She has nothing to give you. She is spent. She has been cheated, abused, used and attacked. It is her turn. The helper stands ready to reach out, to be there through thick and thin and has so much insight to offer. The problem is that a victim may not be able to care. She may not care enough to say thank you, to heed advice, to follow directions and may directly sabotage your efforts. She goes back to her trafficker time and again, putting herself in harm's way, only to beg you to give her another chance when she is beaten once again.

This dance is one sided. And remains that way until it's not. And then it becomes that way again. This is draining work.

As professionals, we are educated and trained to hear the stories. We know the dynamics of the problem, the cycle of abuse and of power and control. We have learned about the importance of life balance and we come out of school ready to hit the streets to help the vulnerable.

That day in school when the professor discussed how it really was going to be, how it was going to mess with your family life, how hard it would be to put your client's crisis before your kid's bedtime story, you must have been absent. You don't always remember hearing that part.

Or maybe you did. Maybe you studied Compassion Fatigue and Burnout and how to avoid it. Take care of yourself, eat right, get enough sleep, exercise and get a hobby. Develop relationships outside of work. Be active spiritually. Oh, maybe you were present that day and learned about it. Maybe this just wasn't going to apply to you. You were different, you know how to handle yourself. Right? Right.?

Until it hits you. You have been tired for the past two years. You numb out when you have to hear the story of gang rape each day. You find yourself looking over your shoulder, wondering if the car behind you is a gang tail. Is that person on the corner following you? A victim returns to her trafficker and is missing. You know she is dead. And you realize you are just moving on. Crossing her off the list. You start having frustrating conversations with collaborative professionals and wonder why they are so darn stupid or lazy. You are too tired to meet colleagues after work. You hear your work cell phone ringing, when it's not.

Calling in sick and cancelling appointments seems more and more like a good idea. You wonder if you are turning into a real true life zombie. You are not even feeling anymore. You can't even cry.

It has happened. You have become a trauma victim yourself. Damn.

In this work, it is not a matter of IF you are going to suffer symptoms of Secondary Traumatic Stress. It is a matter of WHEN and how fast you will catch it or respond when someone else mentions it.

Compassion Fatigue
Compassion Fatigue is a trendy word these days. All the cool kids are getting it. The Sunday paper has stories about how burnout is the name of the game in today's world.

Compassion Fatigue is really a term used to describe a series of conditions of varying degrees of severity, all with similar but distinctly different symptoms.

Under the general heading of Compassion Fatigue lies Burnout, Secondary Traumatic Stress and Vicarious Trauma. As a professional working with trafficking victims it is vital you learn about each of these conditions. You are at very high risk for all of them. They are REAL!

Burnout
Burnout is the level of negative effect that the environment has on you.

Burnout is often directly related to your circumstances as an employee. The inability to make something happen for a client, bureaucratic processes that impede your ability to help, paperwork, and workload all contribute to burn out. Other sources of burnout are: unbending rules in the workplace (have you ever been on your way to search for a runaway victim only to be told to wear more appropriate "workplace attire?"), unfairness in structure or a demanding boss, low morale from your peers, criticism after you have worked really hard but had a difficult outcome.

Burnout is often described as an ongoing state that occurs over time and the contributing factors include not only the individual but also the population served and the organization. There are three specific areas of burnout which include, "emotional exhaustion, depersonalization, and reduced sense of personal accomplishment" (Newell & MacNeil, 2010, p. 59).

Symptoms of burnout are fatigue, never-ending fatigue. Feelings of helplessness, negative attitudes about work that grow into negative attitudes about most people or life in general, frequent absenteeism from work, low completion rates in clinical and administrative duties, emotional exhaustion. (Bara,, Nissly, & Levin, Maslach & Leiter 1997, Shackelford 2006)

Burnout is very real. Dealing with it requires some extensive time off and professional support to take a break. Moving to another part of the organization after a vacation may be most beneficial. Taking a lower caseload for a while may also be helpful. Finding a new, yet supportive, supervisor not directly in charge of your work or coach may also be necessary to help you reframe the work.

What is important is that you deal with burnout if you find yourself having symptoms. Burnout does not just pass. It grows, it festers and it takes a toll on you physically and emotionally. You will not be successful in the helping profession if you do not deal with it directly and head on. As a professional working with trafficking victims, if you do not address symptoms of burnout quickly and aggressively, you will become the grand prize winner of a full-blown case of Secondary Traumatic Stress Disorder. This is the even less fun sister of Burnout. You will not like her.

It is also important to know that trauma informed organizations can find ways to support you to help you avoid burnout. For example, trauma informed organizations make sure that the workload is manageable and that you can be "done" at the end of the day. These organizations take Supervision seriously and provide training to supervisors to teach how they can relieve some of the day to day burden, provide support to barrier busting, to allow you to speak your truth openly and to really listen, to implement some of your ideas and solutions and to provide a good balance between support and structure.

A trauma informed organization will also provide a mechanism for you to get support. This can take the form of an Employee Assistance Program or funding for short term treatment from a community provider. A really good trauma informed organization will contract with a skilled and knowledgeable provider in all forms of Compassion Fatigue and create a "no barriers" access to treatment.

Secondary Traumatic Stress
One does not have to be burned out to catch the Secondary Traumatic Stress (STS) bug. It is a brutal side-effect of the work. Professionals working with trauma victims are far more likely to experience STS symptoms. Burnout creeps in. STS might creep in but also might fall upon you like a ton of bricks one bright and sunny afternoon.

Secondary trauma, often referred to as Vicarious Trauma, is the cumulative and damaging effects that happen to clinicians after they are chronically exposed to their clients' traumatic stories. (Michalopoulos & Aparicio, 2011). STS can mimic the symptoms of Post Traumatic Stress Disorder and STS can blossom into full blown PTSD.

STS is considered to be a result of indirect trauma exposure. The trauma did not happen to you, but listening to the details from a client you care about and wish to help can become traumatizing. The symptoms of STS can include the symptoms of burnout, but go beyond burnout emotional fatigue, depersonalization and a reduced sense of accomplishment. STS symptoms can include: recollections, dreams and reminders of the event causing anxiety or physical reactions, avoidance of thoughts or feelings, gaps in memory, intrusive thoughts; feeling estranged from others; feeling flat, or emotional numbness, feeling hopelessness, trouble sleeping or staying asleep, outburst of anger or irritability, difficulty concentrating, hypervigilance, exaggerated startle response, or having thoughts of violence against the perpetrator. (Adapted from Pryce, Shackeford, & Price, 2007; Occupational Hazards of Work in Child Welfare) Clinicians that work with trauma may also experience decreased capacity to trust their instincts, think highly of themselves and/or be comfortable being alone. (Way, VanDeusen, & Cottrell, 2007)

Vicarious Trauma
Vicarious Trauma is often thought of as the same thing as STS. Some researchers see a difference. Vicarious Trauma is described as the negative transformation of self that occurs as a result of empathy towards the client and the desire to "fix it" or a sense of responsibility to help. (Figley 1995) Vicarious Trauma can make boundaries more difficult to maintain with clients and result in a diminished view of the world. It can also be described as becoming crabby or cynical.

What is important to remember is that these psychological conditions are a result of the helper working with victims of trauma and is a response to hearing trauma details from others. By mislabeling what is psychologically happening to a helping professional it can lead to the helper leaving the field or continuing on in the field but in an impaired way. Unfortunately, many direct care professionals seek to relieve their symptoms by becoming Supervisors. This only perpetuates a negative cycle of the burned out clinicians attempting to help the burned out therapists. The personal and professional distortions that happen with each psychological state are different but influence the helping professional's ability to be clear headed, compassionate and objective in the work.

Direct Trauma

Another important consideration is that there are two primary types of trauma exposure helping professionals face. Direct trauma is a very real consequential hazard of working in the helping professions. Direct trauma does not necessarily mean violence in the overt physical sense. It includes more subtle forms of abuse such as name calling, cursing, insults, verbal threats, and property damage. This type of violence can be just as negatively impactful on the helper as direct violence. One incident of tire slashing can send feelings of rage, fear and trauma into overdrive. Over time, we become numb to clients becoming verbally abusive, but becoming numb is not a good thing. It leads to burnout quickly. In an effort to protect oneself from direct trauma, the helper begins to increasingly put up a guarded persona of protection that influences the ability to be truly present and in the moment with clients.

Helping professionals must not only cope with clients demonstrating dysregulated mood and behavior (a professional way to describe volatile, unpredictable and ungrateful clients), they are also often working in unsupportive and demanding work environments. The work environment itself becomes emotionally hazardous as supervisors inadvertently create a "toughen up and get over it" culture of minimizing direct trauma events. When the "system" stops working to support helpers or the clients, they are assisting, clients begin to experience the frustration and lack of genuine caring. They begin to act out. Supervisors experience their own trauma as a result of staff shortages, resignations and lack of funding. This cycle of trauma and abuse takes over, making trauma informed care impossible.

Indirect Trauma

There are more pressures placed upon helping professionals in addition to the acting out behaviors of clients. We have discussed the impact of hearing traumatic experiences from clients. There are many other ways that helping professionals become exposed to stressors that result in Burnout or STS.

Workloads are notoriously large in the helping professions across the country. First responders are expected to perform heroic acts daily in the face of mass shootings, raging forest fires and hurricanes. Law Enforcement must ensure their own safety when a simple traffic stop could mean bullets will be directed at them. They must discern in a split second when to shoot or when to stand down in the face of life threatening danger. Child Protective Services workers must visit homes that may have meth labs or active opioid use. Gangs rule many communities in the nation, threatening anyone who does not support their agenda. Nurses face increased responsibilities in a system that expects patients to be saved no matter the medical challenge, and yet hospitals are expected to discharge patients following major surgery in a matter of a day. These challenges are real. Funding is down. Support is down. The media is watching for any opportunity for a story to sensationalize tragedy.

Threat of media exposure can in and of itself exacerbate symptoms of STS. Foster Care workers are not only concerned with the safety and well-being of children. They must protect the needs of a child within a system of intense regulations, mandates and Court oversight. With large caseloads and thousands of youth in the foster care system throughout the country, foster care workers are forced to think about the consequences of a bad outcome that will be blamed directly on them as a result. When unfortunate tragedy strikes and a child is maltreated by a foster family, the focus immediately is on worker involvement. Why didn't the worker visit more often, didn't she notice the foster parents had issues? Why did she not make daily visits? Why didn't she stop parent visits? Media attention seldom is on high caseloads, Court rulings, mandated reunification plans, foster parent shortages or the myriad of other systemic issues that are often the root cause of such a tragedy.

Tragedies become front page news and are highly personalized. This is true when a helper acts heroically or when there is an unanticipated outcome. Names are printed, privacy is violated. In an instant, a helping professional must face the possibility of being vilified in the media. Systems often respond to this pressure by increased requirements, more paperwork and tighter auditing processes. Community perceptions of an agency or an entire profession can be impacted by one situation. Politicians who may or may not know the facts hold news conferences. Each individual helping professional must wonder if today it will be her turn to be thrown into the limelight.

Burnout and STS in the Supervisor
Central to the prevention of burnout and STS is the importance of compassionate and regular supervision for the helping professional. As will be discussed later, helpers must have a place to seek support, understanding and structure when in traumatizing (direct or indirect) situations.

What happens when the Supervisor is suffering from burnout and/or STS? Supervisors have an increased risk of STS. Often, direct field helpers seek supervisory positions in an effort to find relief from direct and indirect trauma. And while it may be true that a Supervisor is exposed to fewer incidents of direct exposure, the indirect exposure continues in the supervisory activity with helpers. Supervisors have an increased risk of STS as they often find themselves responsible for putting unrealistic pressures on those they supervise due to staff shortages and high caseloads. Supervisors may inadvertently find themselves the administrator of trauma in an attempt to "keep the ship afloat." Feelings of shame, guilt and grief can easily cloud the Supervisors ability to cope. "Ignoring Supervisors' response to the stressful and often painful work they do puts the entire system at risk" (Crystal Collins-Camargo). In one study supervisors and managers had a 49% rate of serious STS symptoms. (Regehr, Chau, Leslie & Howe, 2002)

Burnout and STS in Foster Parents
Foster Parents get a special shout out in the STS discussion because they are often forgotten professionals who do so much for so little. These heroes take on the most extreme challenges presented by troubled or traumatized children. They are expected to meet the complex needs of youth who have been battered and bruised. They risk their own safety by doing so. Foster Parents see the restless nights, the fears and the emotional consequences of trauma. They hear the horrific stories of these vulnerable victims in the middle of a nightmare. When a child victim has a rage response to trauma, it is the Foster Parent's personal home and items that get damaged. They are on duty twenty four hours, seven days a week. They do not get

holidays. They rarely get respite. In return, Foster Parents receive little financial compensation, limited support and function as key participants in an overloaded system that is often understaffed, and under resourced.

Diagnosing Oneself
Attempting to diagnose oneself is, as you know, never a good idea. You may be like many people who read a symptom and immediately imagine that is the exotic disease you have. Somehow you remember being bitten by that rattlesnake, even though you have been nowhere near any form of snake, the reptilian kind anyway. On the other hand, you may be fooled into thinking you can handle things, you are emotionally stronger than the others, and that you have a calling. We can all fool ourselves when trying to figure out our own issues. That said, it may be helpful to know how to do some self-checking to make sure all is well emotionally.

As mentioned earlier in this chapter, it is sometimes difficult to understand what the difference is between burnout and STS. One way is to ask yourself (or your supervisee), "When did you start feeling this way?" If the response is "I don't know, it feels like I have always felt this way" or "a long time, it just crept up on me and one day I realized I was spent." That is a burnout response.

When looking for a way to differentiate a burnout response from STS ask the same question, "When did you start feeling this way?" and if the response is more like "I started feeling this way after I worked the Annie case" or "I knew I was in trouble when the Suzie case kept me up at night." then that is a symptom of STS creeping in. (Pryce et al., 2007) The severity of STS is dependent on the intensity and extent of your symptoms. The more Post Traumatic Stress Disorder symptoms you experience, the more severe your situation.

Now What Do We Do About This?
So, here we are. You may be asking yourself "Why did I decide to be a helping professional instead of an accountant or a fashion model?" You wanted to make a difference. (You do!) You wanted to help people. (You do!) You wanted to support and heal the most vulnerable victims. (You do!) You were drawn to helping trafficking victims for the adrenalin rush. (Get that.) So, here we are.

Prevention

Certainly, you have heard about the importance of self-care and mindfulness. If you get focused on the prevention of Burnout and STS from day one, you have a fighting chance to prevent yourself from falling victim to these issues. Yet all the self-care in the universe will not ensure you will not catch this bug. It is insidious and tenacious. Self-care will absolutely help you stay healthy, but sometimes the bug gets you anyway.

So, let's talk about some strategies. If you are reading this book, you are a helping professional that has or is contemplating diving off the cliff into the abyss of Compassion Fatigue waters. There are very large and scary sharks in those waters. You have much to do to protect yourself!

The ultimate solution is to BUILD RESILIENCE!

That sounds so easy. (Insert eye roll here.) Eric Gentry, PhD., has done extensive research on the prevention and treatment of Compassion Fatigue. In his work, he quotes the great author Victor Frankel frequently. Victor Frankel is a holocaust survivor and author of the classic book "Man's Search for Meaning." One quote from Mr. Frankel is especially poignant:

"Between stimulus and response, there is a space. In that space is our power to choose our response. In our response lies our growth and our freedom." (Frankel 1997)

Mr. Frankel is referencing surviving the German concentration camps during World War II. Yet, his words resonate for those in the helping professions of modern day. We have a choice. We can take action to stay healthy, build resilience and fight like heck to avoid the STS bug bite. Those of us that have already been bitten can also take action to get healthy once again and make whatever modifications are necessary to rebuild and resume one's chosen profession. The alternative is to quit and become a video game programmer or a dermatologist. Great professions, more money, regular hours, predictable days. You even help people! After you have thought that over, if you have decided to continue to work with the vulnerable, read on.

To prevent STS completely, you must take a holistic approach that includes examination and action within oneself and a close examination of the workplace and action within that environment as well.

Prevention within the Organization

Workers may have more influence within an organization than they believe. The push for helping organizations to become Trauma Informed is on the rise. Federal grants require it, the research on the impact of Adverse Childhood Events supports it and workforce shortages in the helping professions motivate organizations to pay attention to it.

As you seek employment, you will want to insist that you work for a Trauma Informed Organization. That designation means more than saying they recognize trauma as important. It means the everyone within the organization, from top management to the housekeeping staff, understand, respect, acknowledge and value the effects of working with trauma survivors. Not only does the organization seek every opportunity to support the victims of trauma, the organization seeks every opportunity to support those that work with the victims of trauma. The more an organization weaves these values into the everyday environment, the more you want to work with that organization. Just say "no" to organizations that support large caseloads without emotional compensation, high turnover numbers (that is a big clue), or random or lackadaisical supervision practices.

In your initial interview, be sure to ask questions such as "How is your organization trauma informed?" Listen to the answers. If the response is "Yes, we are." Without elaboration, get suspicious. A trauma informed organization will list all the things they do to actively support victims and staff. They will be proud of their investment in staff and will be able to articulate their efforts, even where they have challenges. You want to work with an organization that is working on it. Ask questions about supervision. If the response is "We have an open door policy" get suspicious. If the answer is "We require a minimum of 30 minutes of formal supervision for every staff member, every week," that is a better response. Find out the training opportunities the organization provides to prevent STS. Ask how the organization seeks to ensure safety for staff (this is especially important when working with trafficking victims and/or domestic violence.) How are workloads managed? What kind of counseling activities are available outside the organization but supported by the organization? How is on-call handled or emergencies? Does the work environment look like fun? It should. All of these questions will not only let you know about the organization, the interviewer will understand that you really know what you are talking about when you say you are "trauma informed".

Prevention for Supervisors
Earlier we discussed how supervisors have an increased risk for STS. We also discussed how direct care staff often seek supervisory positions to get relief from field work. This puts the whole system of caring at risk. In the end, victims don't get the help they need and helping professionals do not get the support they need. Bad things can happen!

To have a Trauma Informed Organization, support for the Supervisor is a must. Implementing a STS prevention strategy without first implementing the same strategy to support supervisors is futile. It must be a parallel process. Supervisors need all of the same supports that field workers do. They need training on self care, they need peer or clinical consultation support and they need to be able to debrief with their peers too. They need involvement in decision making at the upper management level and support and recognition for the challenges of implementing constant policy changes, workforce and turnover issues, as well as the never ending paperwork they are responsible to make sure is completed timely and well. A burned out supervisor will not help anyone and may even negatively impact client care. Supervisors must have time on their schedule to be thoughtful, mindful, organized and purposeful. Without that, they will be forced to make snap decisions when workers need answers in a crisis.

Keeping Yourself Sane
Find that space. Remember the quote from Victor Frankel? "Between stimulus and response there is a space. In that space lies our power to choose our response. In our response lies our growth and our freedom." Get Zen about it. We choose our life. We don't always choose what happens in life, but we do choose our response to what happens. Get clear about how you think life works. Are you reactive

to difficult personal situations? Do your feelings and internal responses overwhelm you and cause you to act a certain way? Or do you choose how to respond to difficult personal situations. Do you understand that you ultimately decide how you are going to act? If you are not clear on these issues, you are not ready to work with trafficking victims. Do the interpersonal work necessary to find your own spiritual space. Get really clear and empowered about your right to be in charge of your life. Make your actions decisions, not reactions. This is fundamental to all the rest.

Keep yourself safe. You know that a sense of safety is a primary need for all of us. You are not an exception. When working with victims of trafficking, it is especially important. Pay attention to safety issues. Take them seriously. Don't compromise. Implement all recommended safety protocols each and every day. Stay vigilant. Along with the safety protocols, learn additional skills. They can become part of your workout routine. Learn how to protect yourself. The more skills you have, the more you can relax and trust your gut to tell you when you are in danger. If you worry about being in danger all of the time, you will miss those key signals. Read "The Gift of Fear" by Galvin de Becker. Great book about living safely.

Be physically healthy. Whatever it is that it means for you. If your immune system weakens, stress will push you over the edge. While we are all aware that eating right and exercise is a good thing, it is especially important when working with trauma. Do your best, but do not get down on yourself if you fall short. Instead, get help. Find support. Participate in alternative health therapies as you need to. Get regular massages, do acupuncture, get facials, whatever makes you feel like you are important.

Find a way to release endorphins. Exercise is good.

Put the oxygen mask on yourself first. If you start to feel fatigue that is not cured in one night's sleep, stop, and figure out what is happening. Don't wait until you have been tired for a week. Your body will tell you what it needs if you listen to it. One late night in the field can mess you up for a long time if you don't regroup. Be selfish about your time. Put your all into work, but make sure you can also have the time to refresh and regroup. If you are feeling tired, ask yourself why. If you don't know the answer, that is your sign. If you are not able to find the answer or solution, immediately seek supervision. Do not pass go. Do not go around the board one more time. Be active in making sure you don't go down that road. There is nothing but trouble there.

Set boundaries. One danger in the helping profession is that crisis' don't happen on a schedule. You are not able to schedule crises on Wednesdays only. They happen in the night, weekends and when your little sister is getting married. They for sure happen if you try to go to the movies. The more you protect your "life time" from your "work time" the better able you will be to stay on track. Get dramatic about it. Develop relationships at work of course, but have most if not all of your really best relationships outside of work. Don't share everything at work, maintain some privacy. You do not have to be an open book in the workplace. Take care not to place too much of "who you are" or feelings of self-worth into the work you do. This can be tricky. The world gives you secondary gain from being a helping professional. If people start saying things to you like "You are amazing, I don't know how you do it!" in social gatherings, this is your sign. You are not your work. Work is not your life. It may be a lifestyle for you, but it must not become your life. If you let it, you are doomed.

Figure out the meaning of life. Find your spiritual reason for working in the helping profession and what your higher calling is. If you know the "why" it is easier to hang in there when challenges present and things get difficult. Participate in a supportive community that support your spiritual perspective. Get clear about the bigger picture of the Universe. Figure out why things happen and how they happen. This leads to the next recommendation…

Be in therapy if you need to be. If graduate school did not propel you screaming into therapy then look at it this way. Why would you not be a recipient of the services your profession provides? Working with trafficking victims will trigger every single solitary issue you have ever had or even thought about having. Period. You have to get clear in your head. No choice. Work for an organization that will pay for it or provides insurance that will.

Insist on quality supervision. This is different than therapy. Supervision is work related support and guidance. Therapy is you focused support and guidance. Quality supervision should focus on how to conceptualize cases, to learn professional techniques and skills, and to process how things are going in the workplace. Your Supervisor should be more qualified than you and know what he or she is dong. A good supervisor is wise. It is important to have a Supervisor that understands that his/her role is to work on your behalf, not the other way around. Quality supervision should focus on how you are managing things, but not on checking off the boxes of did you get this done or that done (unless that is structure you want and need to feel accountable.) Your Supervisor's office should be your work "safe place". It should be a place to vent (so you don't have to do that with peers,) to safely share concerns, opinions and ideas. It should be a place to come to and just breathe. If needed, your Supervisor should have the wisdom of knowing when to step out and let you stay and get quiet time. If you are not getting that on a scheduled basis, and as needed. Fix that fast!

Establish a "got your back" work culture. Be part of the team. Participating in a work environment of mutual respect and camaraderie is so fun and rewarding. Trusting that if you make a mistake or start to drift, someone will help you out and pull you to safety. This is a vital part of psychological safety. The work is difficult and victims of trafficking can be frustrating. Having a Team approach makes it so much easier. Peer interaction does not take the place of good Supervision, but having complete support and the opportunity to help your team by giving your complete support makes going to work better.

Following these helpful tips will not ensure you do not catch the STS bug but they sure will help. They will set the stage to stave off burnout, which will leave you stronger and more resilient if the STS bug bites. The key is to really understand that this is an active process. The organization you work for has responsibilities, but so do you. It is your choice to participate in the helping professions. Along with that come some tools of your craft. These Resilience Tools are as important to you as a screwdriver is to an electrician. Take developing these tools seriously. They matter.

CONCLUSION

When we wrote this book, the intention was really to educate. As we started to research and started to do more focus on our perceptions and the need as it relates to gang-controlled sexual exploitation, we started to look at a bunch of different things. At first, we thought that we should write about a victim in a truly diverse manner. We can share thousands of stories and make people cry by the challenges our clients face. However, we are not magicians and cannot make people passionate, educated and dedicated to the issue. The poetry hits to the real core and reality of the true victimization, perceptions, and mentality.

We hope through the stories and information that it makes you think about how many people have come into Veronica's life. From her family to school professionals, business owners, mental health practitioners, law enforcement, social workers, gas station attendants, daycare providers, or other public and private sectors. How many people have believed something was wrong but didn't ask? Thought that someone else would address it or report it? Thought that she would never make it? Now, how many of us can look back and say something was wrong.

For Veronica, her ability to overcome, ask for help, advocate for herself and have hope related to her success.

Never in her life did Veronica ever imagine being a college student struggling in her math class. Never did she imagine talking to someone that knows of the most traumatic parts of her about needing math to help her with "Big Girl Problems." When you're looking in perceptively and you hear about Veronica's story and now being a college student, the hope is that it makes you look differently when understanding gangs and gang-controlled exploitation victims.

Veronica's story is very similar to many stories. Her story of childhood trauma, neglect, lack of fatherly figure, substance-abuse, gang involvement, negative peer association, and numerous professionals coming in and out of her life, but over everything, her ability to overcome. Veronica is a full-time student at a prestigious university, a mother, and also works part-time.

If you interact with or see her, you will never know what she has been through, what she has overcome, no identifying marks, and does not wear tattoos. She is a student, a mother, a friend, and family member.

SPECIAL THANKS

Words can express how much support I had for this book. Special thanks for the amazing artwork and poetry.

Aaron R Poems
All of the amazing poetry was specifically put together and shaped together by Aaron R. His other work can be found at aaronRpoems.com. Aaron also published *Poetically Correct*

McKenzie Wilson
All of the artwork on the interior of the book was completed by McKenzie Wilson. McKenzie is a talented artist and was able to capture the intricate details of gang controlled sexual exploitation through her drawing.

Amy Barrow Jones
The artwork on the front cover was completed by Amy Barrow Jones. Her additional artwork can be found at axtattoo.com

TRAUMA AND HOPE

Trauma and Hope was formed by Deepa Patel and Pablo Moro. They are licensed clinical social workers (LCSW) and Certified Sex Offender Treatment Providers (CSOTP). Deepa and Pablo are considered senior clinicians and have contracted with numerous county, private and non-profit agencies for many years. Through years of experience, Trauma and Hope was formed and provides specialized assessments and treatment for children, adolescents, families, and adults as well as consultation and training. Clinicians at Trauma and Hope have expertise in the following areas: trauma informed care, sexually acting out, mood disorders, anger management and substance abuse/use. The treatment methodology comes from a holistic philosophy using evidence-based approaches and interventions.

For more information visit traumaandhope.com

THE RESILIENCE NETWORK

The Resilience Network provides an evidenced-based approach to resilience skill building that is action-oriented using multiple modalities. Rather than diagnosing and relitigating problems through traditional psychotherapy, we help our clients to find productive ways to problem-solve and interact with the world around them. The Resilience Network has developed a new, action-based modality to educate clinicians, organizations, and individuals on how best to strategize and implementation of appropriate interventions and services.

For more information visit Resilience-network.net

REFERENCES

Carnes, Patrick, *The Betrayal Bond,* (1997), Health Communications Inc. Deerfield Beach, Florida.

Curran, Linda A. *101 Trauma-Informed Interventions* (2013). Pesi, Wisconsin.

Curran, Linda A. *Trauma Competency: A Clinician's Guide* (2010). Pesi. Wisconsin.

Dutton, D.G., & Painter, S.L. (1981). Traumatic Bonding: The development of emotional attachments in battered women and other relationships of intermittent abuse. Victimology, 6, 139 155.

Harris, M., and Tallot, R. D., (Eds) (2001) *Using Trauma Theory to Design Service Systems: New Directions for Mental Health Services*, New York: Jossey-Bass.

Herman, Judith Lewis, *Trauma and Recovery: The Aftermath of Violence-from Domestic Abuse To Political Terrorism,* (1992), Basic Books: New York.

Hossain, M., Zimmerman, C., Abas, M., Light, M., and Waltz, C., *The Relationship of Trauma To Mental Disorder Among Trafficked and Sexually Exploited Girls and Women*, Journal of Public Health, 100 (12).

Julian D. Ford (2015) *Complex PTSD: Research Directions for Nosology/Assessment, Treatment, and Public Health*, European Journal of Psychotraumatology, 6:1, 27584, DOI: 10.3402/ejpt.v6.27584

Mattar, Mohamed Y. "Interpreting Judicial Interpretations of the Criminal Statutes of the Trafficking Victims Protection Act: Ten Years Later." American University Journal of Gender Social Policy and Law 19, no. 4 (2011): 1247-1304.

Marano, Hara Estroff, and Carlin Flora. 2004, September 1. "The Truth About Compatibility." *Psychology Today.* http://www.psychologytoday.com/articles/200411/the-truth-about-compatibility.

Marazziti, Donatella, Hagop S. Akiskal, Alessandra Rossi, and Giovanni B. Cassano. 1999. "Alteration of the Platelet Serotonin Transporter in Romantic Love." *Psychological Medicine* 29: 741- 45.

Najavits, Lisa M, *Seeking Safety: A Treatment Manual for PTSD and Substance Abuse* (2002), The Guilford Press. New York,

Naperstek, Belleruth, *Invisible Heroes, Survivors of Trauma and How They Heal, (*2007), Bantam Books, New York,

Priebe, A. S., C. (2005). Hidden in Plain View: The commercial sexual exploitation of girls in Atlanta. Atlanta, Georgia: The Atlanta Women's Agenda.

Smith, J. A., Flowers, P., & Larkin, M. (2009). Interpretative phenomenological analysis: Theory, method and research. London, UK: Sage.

Van der Kolk, Bessel, McFarlane, A.C., and Weisaeth, L. (Eds), 1996, *Traumatic Stress,* Guilford Press, New York.